FOUR SEASONS
SALADS

FOUR SEASONS
SALADS

Jackie Burrow

CONTENTS

This edition first published 1988 by
Hamlyn Publishing Group
Michelin House
81 Fulham Road
London SW3 6RB

© 1984 Hennerwood Publications Limited

ISBN 0 600 55882 7

Printed in Hong Kong

INTRODUCTION

Gone are the days when salads were only served on hot summer days, and always consisted of lettuce, tomato and cucumber. Now salads are served all the year round and include numerous exciting ingredients, depending on the seasonal food available. Salads can be served for all sorts of occasions and can range from substantial main courses to colourful side dishes and sophisticated starters. They may be simple to prepare, requiring only a few minutes to assemble before serving, or they may involve more elaborate preparations in advance.

Whichever type of salad you choose, it will always be fun to put together as salads invariably consist of contrasting flavours, colours and textures. Preparing a salad is a wonderful excuse to indulge your imagination in the way you arrange the ingredients and in trying out new garnishes. The presentation of a salad is all important and it is fun to look out for interesting plates and dishes to serve them on (wooden salad bowls are perfect for green salads, but do not show off more elaborate salads to an advantage). Many salads look prettiest when arranged on individual dishes.

The recipes in this book are arranged according to the four seasons of the year. In each season you will find a selection of recipes for starters, main courses and side salads, including a few vegetarian salads. The inspiration for the recipes has been drawn from all over the world, giving them a wide variety of flavour and feel, and introducing lots of new ideas on combining and presenting familiar and exotic ingredients.

As all the ingredients are fresh and seasonal, all the salads are healthy and nutritious and some of them will be ideal for slimmers (although watch out for calorie-laden ingredients such as cheese, nuts, avocados and oily dressings). As there's seldom a need to worry about keeping a salad hot it's an excellent choice for entertaining, as well as for feeding the family.

Salad Dressings

The dressing is a vitally important element of any salad, and can literally make or break a salad's success. There are numerous different types of dressing; choose one according to the ingredients you have available and the salad it is destined to dress. The classic French dressing (or vinaigrette) must be made with the best quality oil and vinegar (do not expect a dressing made from malt vinegar and cooking oil to taste nice!). The exact proportions will depend on the types of oil and vinegar used, so this dressing should therefore always be made to taste. A good vinaigrette is indispensable if you make salads regularly, and it's a good idea to make up a large quantity at a time and store it in a screw-top jar. Remember to shake the jar vigorously before you use it, and do not keep a dressing for longer than one week. Mayonnaise is another classic dressing which can be served with most salads, and homemade mayonnaise always tastes totally different from shop-bought varieties.

All sorts of other ingredients may be used in salad dressings. Yogurt, soured cream, cheeses, honey, sugar, garlic, herbs, citrus and other fruit juices are just a few; it's fun to experiment with different combinations.

Delicate fresh green salad leaves should be dressed just before serving, as they wilt if left sitting in a dressing. The more robust green and root vegetables can be dressed in advance, indeed this is often necessary to allow them to soften and develop a better flavour by marinating for a while. Starchy salad ingredients such as potatoes, rice, pasta and pulses all benefit from being dressed straight after cooking while still hot so that they can absorb the flavour of the dressing.

Recipes for Mayonnaise, French dressing and other salad dressings can be found on pages 78-9.

Spring

Spring is the season when the days grow warmer and one begins to think of serving salads, and also perhaps of eating lighter meals to shed any extra pounds that might have crept on during the winter months. Spring, however, is often the most difficult time of year to find salad ingredients, either in the shops or in the vegetable garden. The home-grown, common salad vegetables like lettuce, cucumber and tomato are not ready for eating yet, and only expensive greenhouse and imported varieties can be found. Fortunately, there are other vegetables available at this time to make delicious salads with, in particular globe artichokes and asparagus, which are at their best in the spring. These two extravagant vegetables make luxurious salads if cooked simply and served cold with mayonnaise or French dressing, but they can also be combined in smaller quantities with other ingredients to make a more economical salad.

In early spring, when there are few salad leaves

around, make use of root vegetables and green leaf vegetables such as cabbage, spring greens and cauliflower. These are not usually associated with salads but are excellent either raw or lightly cooked and served in interesting dressings. Pulses are another useful standby when fresh vegetables are scarce and expensive. Haricot beans, black-eye beans, butter beans, kidney beans and lentils all make delicious cheap starters and side salads when cooked and combined with contrasting ingredients and a good salad dressing. Sprouts from beans are another valuable addition to salads when other vegetables are scarce. Small young spinach leaves can be used raw or lightly cooked to make different and nutritious salads. Other versatile ingredients include avocados, citrus fruits and pineapples. Later in the spring, delicious new potatoes and sweet young carrots increase the repertoire of salad vegetables, both of which can be used without peeling.

Summer

Summer is the time for eating out of doors, picnics and barbecues. As summer approaches all the fresh salad ingredients become cheaper and more plentiful, in particular you will find several varieties of lettuce available such as crisp hearty Webbs Wonderful or the long thick cos types, both of which go a long way and keep well in the refrigerator if covered.

Tomatoes, cucumbers, sweet peppers, aubergines, courgettes and other vegetable fruits start to feature in the shops and in the vegetable garden. These are all delicious additions to salads and can be used raw or cooked, apart from aubergines which must be cooked before eating. Tomatoes in particular are invaluable for evoking a wonderful Mediterranean feel in salads. Summer is also the time for vegetable pods and seeds. Fresh young broad beans and young small peas are excellent raw in salads, as are French and runner beans, larger peas and mangetout, although all of these need to be lightly cooked first. Radishes and beetroots are also ready for picking and make colourful additions to any salad.

Fresh herbs are available throughout the summer and make a tremendous difference to salads. Some, such as parsley, fennel and chives, can be chopped up finely and included as an ingredient or as a garnish. Others, such as basil, sage, dill and marjoram, can be added in smaller quantities to dressings. Many are relatively easy to grow yourself either in the garden or in window boxes (mint, basil, thyme, chives, marjoram, tarragon, parsley).

For more luxurious salads salmon and sea trout can be used, as can soft summer fruits like strawberries, raspberries and melons.

Just a selection of the many salad ingredients available during the spring and summer months

Autumn

Orchard fruits such as apples, pears, plums, peaches and blackberries herald the beginning of autumn, and all of these fruits combine well with savoury foods in salads. The summer fruit vegetables like tomatoes, courgettes, aubergines, peppers and runner beans are also still in good supply early in the autumn. Marrows and corn on the cob are unique to this season and both can be cooked and used as unusual salad components. Mushrooms are available in abundance at this time of year – in the shops and also in the fields, where there are several varieties ready for picking (but do make sure first that they are safe to eat).

Stalk vegetables like celery, Chinese leaves and fennel are plentiful now and are all interesting raw additions to autumn salads. Leeks are also beginning to re-appear in the shops.

With the onset of winter fresh salad leaves and herbs disappear and one has to rely instead on store cupboard ingredients for flavourings and garnishes; capers, gherkins, anchovies, olives of all types, nuts and dried fruits will all liven up any salads, as will the many varieties of grapes available at this time of year.

Winter

Winter sees the return of favourite vegetables which have been absent during the summer months: leeks, onions, red, green and white cabbage, broccoli, cauliflower, Brussels sprouts. Many of these vegetables are best after a frost, and they can be used raw, finely shredded, or lightly cooked.

Root vegetables such as carrot, celeriac, turnip and kohlrabi are also good salad ingredients; grated, finely chopped, or gently cooked. Chicory and endive are great winter salad standbys and can be used instead of lettuce. They both keep well in the refrigerator. Radiccio, a very attractive small red chicory, is an unusual and delicious leaf to add to winter salads (it is expensive, but a little goes a long way).

Jerusalem artichokes tend to be an underrated vegetable, they too are delicious if cooked and added to a salad. Around Christmas there is an excellent supply of fresh nuts: chestnuts, cob nuts, almonds, brazils and walnuts, all of which are good in salads, as are dried fruits, and fresh dates, also available at this time. Citrus fruits are in season, and the tartness of oranges, tangerines and grapefruits makes a good contrast to blander salad ingredients, as do herrings and mussels, which are both good cooked and served cold in salads. Or try imported fruits such as pineapples and cranberries which have distinct and sharp flavours.

Autumn and winter salads require a little ingenuity, but there are many colourful ingredients available to choose from

VEGETABLE CALENDAR

INTRODUCTION 9

Legend:
- HOME GROWN
- IMPORTED
- HOME GROWN AND IMPORTED
- NOT AVAILABLE

Columns (by season/month):
SPRING: March, April, May | SUMMER: June, July, August | AUTUMN: September, October, November | WINTER: December, January, February

Left column vegetables:
- ARTICHOKES globe
- ARTICHOKES Jerusalem
- ASPARAGUS
- AUBERGINES
- AVOCADO PEARS
- BEANS broad
- BEANS French
- BEANS runner
- BEAN-SPROUTS mung
- BEETROOT
- BROCCOLI calabrese (green)
- BROCCOLI purple sprouting
- BRUSSELS SPROUTS
- CABBAGE green
- CABBAGE red
- CABBAGE spring greens
- CABBAGE white
- CARROTS
- CAULIFLOWER
- CELERIAC
- CELERY
- CHICORY
- CHILLI PEPPERS
- CHINESE LEAVES
- COURGETTES
- CUCUMBER
- ENDIVE
- FENNEL
- KOHLRABI

Right column vegetables:
- LEEKS
- LETTUCE Cos
- LETTUCE iceberg
- LETTUCE round
- LETTUCE Webbs
- MARROW
- MUSHROOMS cultivated
- MUSHROOMS field
- MUSTARD AND CRESS
- ONIONS pickling
- ONIONS shallots
- ONIONS Spanish
- ONIONS spring
- PARSNIPS
- PEAS garden
- PEAS mangetout
- PEPPERS
- POTATOES new
- POTATOES old
- PUMPKINS
- RADICCIO
- RADISHES
- SORREL
- SPINACH
- SWEDE
- SWEETCORN
- TOMATOES
- TURNIPS
- WATERCRESS

UNUSUAL VEGETABLES

The following vegetables are unusual in two ways. Either they are not as familiar and widely available as the usual tomato, radish or cucumber, or else they are not normally thought of as ingredients for salads, for example broad beans and cauliflower.

Artichoke – Globe

A member of the thistle family. The fat bases of the leafy 'petals' are edible and the artichoke bottom or 'heart' is considered a delicacy.

Preparation Must be cooked. Cut off stalks to make a level base. Pull off any tough outer leaves and trim the tips of the remaining leaves if preferred. Cook in boiling salted water for 30-40 minutes or until a leaf pulls out easily. Drain upside down until cold. Remove choke. (See page 26.)

Serving ideas Serve as a starter, with Vinaigrette, Mayonnaise or hollandaise sauce to dip the leaf bases into. Hearts can be served on their own or with other ingredients for hors d'oeuvre. 'Cups' (with choke removed) can be stuffed. Artichoke hearts are available in cans.

Artichoke – Jerusalem

A tuber looking like a knobbly potato but with the flavour of artichoke.

Preparation Must be cooked and peeled (either before or after cooking). Discolours easily so submerge in cold water mixed with a little lemon juice or vinegar immediately after peeling. Boil in salted water with a little lemon juice or vinegar added for 10-15 minutes until just tender. Drain and cool.

Serving ideas Slice and toss in a lemon dressing. Mix with Mayonnaise, as for potato salad.

Asparagus

Stalks 6-8 inches long, can be green or white, thin or thick. Tips and most of stalks are edible.

Preparation Must be cooked. Wash, trim off woody ends. The stalks take longer to cook than the tips, so tie in bundles and cook upright, so that the stalks cook in the boiling water while the tips cook in the steam away from the heat source. Cook in boiling salted water (with a little lemon juice added to prevent discolouration) for about 15 minutes.

Serving ideas Can be eaten hot or cold. Serve as a starter with Vinaigrette, Mayonnaise or hollandaise sauce to dip stalks into. Available in cans and frozen.

Aubergine

The large purple variety is the most commonly seen.

Preparation Must be cooked, usually with skin on. Trim off stalk and cut into slices or dice. These are usually sprinkled with salt and left to drain in a colander for 30 minutes to draw out the bitter juices, then rinsed and patted dry before cooking. Bake whole in a medium oven for 30 minutes-1 hour, depending on size, or fry slices or dice until golden brown and tender, about 5 minutes. Leave to cool.

Serving ideas Serve with a Vinaigrette or Yogurt dressing. Purée the pulp of baked aubergines to make a pâté. Include as part of ratatouille; a Provençal vegetable stew.

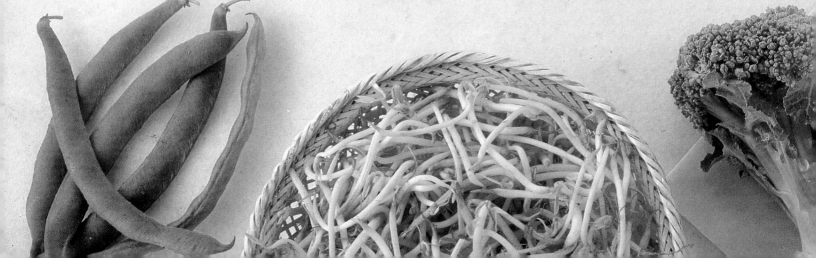

Avocado Pear

A pear-shaped tropical fruit with a dark green skin.
Preparation Use raw. Cut in half with a stainless steel knife and remove the stone. Rub the cut surfaces with lemon juice immediately to prevent discolouration.
Serving ideas Serve unpeeled halves filled with Vinaigrette or prawns in Mayonnaise. Alternatively peel and use in salads sliced or cubed, a little adds an interesting flavour and texture to green salads. Purée to make a pâté or dip.

Beans – Broad

Large lumpish beans in a pod which have a whitish skin and bright green flesh.
Preparation Usually cooked but very young beans may be eaten raw, like peas. Remove from pods and cook in boiling salted water for 5-10 minutes, depending on age, until just tender. Drain and cool.
Serving ideas Serve in a Vinaigrette or Yogurt dressing with herbs. Can be part of an hors d'oeuvre.

Beans – French and Runner

Both varieties are bright green, the French being small, round and thin and the runner long and flat.
Preparation Must be lightly cooked. French beans can usually be topped and tailed and left whole, but may also be cut into pieces. Remove coarse string from length of runner beans, then slice diagonally. Boil in salted water for about 5 minutes until tender but still crisp. Drain and cool.
Serving ideas Serve alone in a dressing, or as part of a composite salad, e.g. salade Niçoise.

Bean-Sprouts

Sprouts from dried beans, usually mung or soya, but virtually any bean can be sprouted (see page 23).
Preparation Wash well. Serve raw.
Serving ideas Good with oriental ingredients.

Broccoli – Calabrese, Purple sprouting

All varieties can be used like cauliflower in salads.
Preparation Serve raw, cut into small pieces, or divide into florets and boil in salted water for 5-10 minutes, depending on the thickness of the stalks, until just tender. Drain and cool.
Serving ideas Serve as starter with hollandaise sauce, or combine with other ingredients in a mixed salad.

Brussels Sprouts

Preparation Serve raw and finely shredded, or boil briefly and cut into halves.
Serving ideas Toss in Vinaigrette or Mayonnaise, as for coleslaw.

Carrots

Carrots are a wonderfully colourful addition to salads, especially winter ones.
Preparation Grate coarsely to serve raw. Serve whole baby carrots raw or very lightly cooked as part of Crudités. Older carrots should be sliced or diced and cooked in boiling water for 10-15 minutes, depending on age and size, until just tender.
Serving ideas Mix grated carrot with French dressing and dried fruits (e.g. currants and raisins). Toss warm cooked carrots in a lemon vinaigrette.

Cauliflower

The white flower heads look attractive in salads.
Preparation Cut into small pieces or divide into florets, and serve raw, or boil in salted water for 5 minutes until just tender, then drain and toss in dressing.
Serving ideas Serve raw florets coated in a spicy dressing, or plain as part of Crudités.

Celeriac

The edible root of a special variety of celery, with a slight celery flavour. A particularly welcome addition to winter salads.
Preparation Must be peeled (toss in lemon juice or Vinaigrette at once to prevent discolouration). Grate, shred or dice and marinate in dressing to soften, or lightly boil shredded or diced celeriac in salted water (for 1 minute if shredded, for up to 5 minutes if diced), drain and toss in dressing while hot.
Serving ideas Traditionally cut into delicate julienne strips and served in a mustard mayonnaise. Blends well with carrot in salads.

Chinese Leaves

The crisp pale coloured leaves are useful in winter salads.
Preparation Wash, shred finely and serve raw. The leaves are rather bland and need a well-flavoured dressing, e.g. prawns, ham, mushrooms.

Courgettes – Green, Yellow and Round

Miniature marrows with a creamy flesh.
Preparation Wash, top and tail. Cut into thin circles or slice lengthways. Serve raw or steam for 5 minutes.
Serving ideas Toss in Vinaigrette or Yogurt dressing.

Fennel

White bulbs with green feathery leaves, a celery-like texture and a slight aniseed flavour.
Preparation Use raw, sliced thinly.
Serving ideas Include as part of Crudités or green salads.

Kohlrabi

White, pale green or purple root vegetable that looks and tastes similar to turnip.
Preparation Peel thickly, cut into slices or dice and cook in boiling salted water for 10-15 minutes until tender. Can also be peeled, grated and served raw.
Serving ideas Toss in French dressing.

Leeks

Very versatile in salads, imparting a mild onion flavour. Can be used whole or sliced, raw or cooked.
Preparation Wash well to remove all dirt. To eat raw, slice thinly and toss in French dressing. Cook whole or sliced in boiling salted water until tender (15 minutes if whole, 3-5 minutes if sliced).
Serving ideas Poach in stock flavoured with a bay leaf, peppercorns, coriander seeds, and lemon.

Lettuce, Endive and Other Salad Leaves

The common varieties of lettuce are : round, cos, Webbs Wonderful and iceberg. The endive family, with a slightly bitter flavour, includes curly endive, batavia, chicory, and radiccio. Dandelion leaves, corn salad, purslane, mustard and cress, sorrel and watercress can also be used.

Preparation Wash and dry well, keep covered in the refrigerator to retain crispness. Dress just before serving as once dressed the leaves quickly go limp.

Serving ideas Toss whole or shredded leaves in a herb-flavoured dressing.

Mangetout Peas

Tender, green vegetables that are eaten pods and all.

Preparation If very small and young, simply top and tail and serve raw. String older mangetout and blanch in well salted water for 1-2 minutes until just tender.

Serving ideas For a starter, mangetout are especially delicious mixed with prawns and a lemon dressing.

Mushrooms

Mushrooms are an excellent source of texture and flavour for salads. They are usually served raw.

Preparation Wipe with a damp cloth or rinse quickly in cold running water. There is no need to peel cultivated mushrooms. Use small succulent button mushrooms whole.

Serving ideas Marinate in dressing with plenty of lemon, combine with seafood for a delicious starter.

Peppers – Green, Red and Yellow

Slices of crisp-textured and strong flavoured raw pepper make colourful additions to salads.

Preparation Remove stalk, core and seeds. Cut into slices or rings. Alternatively, grill until the skins blacken and blister, then rub the skins off under running water.

Serving ideas Halve, stuff and bake. Cut into strips and use as a garnish.

Pulses

Any type of dried pulse may be used in salads.

Preparation Need to be prepared ahead. Soak in water overnight, boil rapidly in clean water for 10 minutes, then cover and simmer for about 1 hour, depending on the type of bean, until tender. Drain and toss in a parsley-flavoured French dressing while still warm so that the flavour is absorbed well.

Serving ideas Combine with seafoods and Vinaigrette for delicious and economical starters. Invaluable in vegetarian salads.

Spinach

Raw, young, small spinach leaves, tossed in dressing, make a delicious salad. Larger spinach stalks may be cooked and served like asparagus.

Preparation Prepare as for Salad leaves.

Serving ideas Traditionally served with a hot bacon dressing as a starter. Add to any mixed green salad as a nutritious change from lettuce.

SPRING

CARIBBEAN PRAWN SALAD

Serves 4 as a light main salad or 6 as a starter
1 small lettuce
2 ripe avocado pears
225 g (8 oz) peeled prawns
8 tablespoons Thousand Island dressing (page 78)
100 g (4 oz) green grapes, halved and seeded
To garnish:
2 tablespoons pumpkin seeds

Preparation time: 10 minutes

1. Wash and dry the lettuce, shred finely and divide between 4 serving plates (or 6 plates if serving as a starter).
2. Halve the avocado pears, remove the stones and peel off the skin. Cut the flesh lengthways into slices and arrange in a fan shape on top of the lettuce.
3. Place the prawns in a mixing bowl and stir in the Thousand Island dressing.
4. Spoon the dressed prawn mixture over the avocado slices and scatter the grapes and pumpkin seeds over. Serve at once.

Variation:
Substitute 1 ripe mango, thinly sliced, for the grapes and interleave between the avocado slices.

NEW POTATO SALAD

Serves 4 as a side salad
750 g (1½ lb) new potatoes, scrubbed
150 ml (¼ pint) Mayonnaise (page 78)
1 tablespoon white wine vinegar
2 spring onions, chopped
1 tablespoon chopped gherkins
1 tablespoon capers
8 small stuffed olives, thinly sliced
freshly ground black pepper
To garnish:
stuffed olives
gherkins

Preparation time: 10 minutes, plus cooling
Cooking time: 15-20 minutes

PINEAPPLE AND WATERCRESS SALAD

Serves 4 as a side salad
100 g (4 oz) watercress
1 small pineapple
50 g (2 oz) walnut halves, roughly chopped
Dressing:
2 tablespoons clear honey
2 tablespoons olive oil
2 tablespoons wine vinegar
salt
freshly ground black pepper

Preparation time: 10 minutes

1. Wash the watercress and remove any coarse stalks. Divide between 4 side plates.
2. Cut the pineapple into 8 thin slices and cut off the skin. Halve each slice and cut out the core.
3. Arrange 4 half slices on each plate and sprinkle with the chopped walnuts.
4. Mix together the dressing ingredients. Pour the dressing over the salad. Serve with any duck dish.

Variation:
Substitute 2 large grapefruit, peeled and sliced, for the pineapple.

1. Put the potatoes in a saucepan and cover with cold water. Bring to the boil and simmer for 10-15 minutes, depending on the size of the potatoes, until cooked but not too soft. Drain and leave to cool.
2. Spoon the mayonnaise into a mixing bowl large enough to hold the potatoes. Stir the vinegar into the mayonnaise, then add the spring onions, gherkins, capers, stuffed olives and pepper. Mix well.
3. If the potatoes are small, leave them whole with their skins on, otherwise cut them into halves or quarters. Add the warm potatoes to the mayonnaise and toss until well coated. Allow to cool. A
4. When ready to serve, turn into a large dish, garnish with stuffed olives and gherkins, and serve with a selection of cold meats.
A Can be made several hours in advance, covered and kept chilled.

Caribbean prawn salad, with mango (TOP) and with grapes (BOTTOM)

BOUILLABAISSE FISH SALAD

Serves 4 as a main salad
1 litre (1¾ pints) water
1 onion, peeled and roughly chopped
1 bay leaf
bunch fresh herbs (parsley, thyme)
1 slice lemon or orange
salt
freshly ground black pepper
500 g (1¼ lb) firm white fish (halibut, turbot, monkfish, squid, etc), cut into large pieces
500 g (1¼ lb) shellfish (mussels, scallops, cooked prawns in shells), cleaned or scrubbed
Rouille mayonnaise:
300 ml (½ pint) Mayonnaise (page 78)
1 × 175 g (6 oz) can pimentos, drained
1 large garlic clove, peeled and crushed
1 tablespoon chopped fresh herbs (basil, thyme, parsley) or 1 teaspoon dried herbs

Preparation time: 30-40 minutes
Cooking time: 15-30 minutes, depending on types of fish used

1. Pour the water into a saucepan and add the onion, bay leaf, herbs, lemon or orange, salt and pepper. Bring to the boil and boil for 5 minutes.
2. Add the white fish and simmer until tender but not broken apart. Remove with a fish slice and leave to cool.
3. Cook the shellfish in the same water. Simmer the shelled scallops for about 5 minutes, then remove and add the scrubbed mussels. Cover the pan and cook until the shells have opened (discard any mussels which do not open).
4. Cut the cold white fish into strips or cubes and arrange in the centre of a serving platter.
5. Arrange the shellfish around the white fish, leaving the mussels in one half of their shells and the prawns in their shells.
6. For the rouille mayonnaise, add the pimento, garlic and herbs to the mayonnaise and liquidize until smooth. Alternatively, pound the ingredients to a paste and stir into the mayonnaise. [A]
7. Serve the fish salad accompanied with the rouille mayonnaise and a green salad.
[A] The rouille mayonnaise can be made up to 2 days ahead, covered and kept chilled.

Variation:
Any combination of fish may be used, as simple or as exotic as you wish. Choose according to what's available and how much you wish to spend. Crab, lobster, clams, crawfish tails – even oysters – can all be included, as can frozen shellfish such as mussels and scallops.

SMOKY FISH AND BEAN SALAD

Serves 4 as a light main salad or 6 as a starter
225 g (8 oz) haricot or black-eye beans, soaked in water overnight, or covered in boiling water and soaked for at least 2 hours
600 ml (1 pint) water
1 small onion, peeled and finely chopped
1 bay leaf
freshly ground black pepper
150 ml (¼ pint) French dressing (page 78)
2 teaspoons creamed horseradish
salt
1 tablespoon chopped fresh parsley
225 g (8 oz) smoked mackerel, skinned and flaked
4 eggs, hard-boiled, shelled and chopped
To serve:
1 lettuce (optional)
twists of lemon
sprigs of parsley

Preparation time: 10 minutes, plus soaking
Cooking time: 1-1¼ hours

1. Place the soaked beans in a saucepan with the water. Add the onion, bay leaf and pepper. Cover and bring to the boil. Boil for 10 minutes, then simmer for 45 minutes-1 hour, until the beans are tender but not mushy. Drain the beans and leave to cool slightly.
2. Mix the French dressing with creamed horseradish, salt and parsley: pour over the beans and stir gently until everything is well coated. [A]
3. Carefully stir in the flaked fish and chopped eggs. Serve at once or cover and chill until required.
4. To serve, arrange the lettuce (if using) in a serving dish or bowl. Pile the bean salad on top of the lettuce and garnish with twists of lemon and parsley sprigs.
[A] Can be made up to 1 day ahead, covered and kept chilled.

FROM THE LEFT Bouillabaisse fish salad; Smoky fish and bean salad

SPRING CARROT SALAD

Serves 4 as a side salad or starter

500 g (1¼ lb) small new carrots, scrubbed
300 ml (½ pint) water
salt
freshly ground black pepper
150 ml (¼ pint) plain unsweetened yogurt
grated rind and juice of ½ orange
2 tablespoons chopped fresh parsley or chives (or a
    mixture of the two)

Preparation time: 10 minutes
Cooking time: about 10 minutes

This salad relies on the sweet flavour of young spring carrots. It's both full of vitamins and low in calories and an excellent choice for slimmers.

1. If the carrots are very small leave them whole, otherwise cut them lengthways into halves or, if they are very squat, into quarters.
2. Place the carrots in a saucepan, pour the water over and add salt and pepper. Bring to the boil and simmer for 5-10 minutes until the carrots are cooked but still crunchy. Drain and leave to cool.
3. For the dressing, mix the yogurt with the orange rind, orange juice and chopped parsley or chives. Add salt and pepper to taste.
4. Place the cold carrots on a serving dish and pour the dressing over. If preparing the salad for a starter, arrange on individual plates. [A]
5. Serve at once, or cover and chill until required. This salad goes well with cold meats, especially gammon and ham.
[A] Can be prepared several hours in advance, covered and kept chilled.

SALAMI, HARICOT AND TOMATO SALAD

Serves 4 as a main salad or 6-8 as a starter
225 g (8 oz) dried haricot beans
600 ml (1 pint) water
450 g (1 lb) tomatoes
1 tablespoon chopped fresh sage or 1 teaspoon dried sage
1 small onion, peeled and chopped
100-175 g (4-6 oz) thinly sliced salami
Dressing:
6 tablespoons reserved cooking juice
1 tablespoon wine vinegar
1 tablespoon olive oil
salt
freshly ground black pepper
sprig of fresh sage leaves, to garnish

Preparation time: 15 minutes, plus soaking
Cooking time: 1-1½ hours

LENTIL AND TOMATO SALAD

Serves 4-6 as a side salad
225 g (8 oz) green lentils
1 small onion, peeled and finely chopped
900 ml (1½ pints) water
1 bay leaf
salt
6 tablespoons French dressing (page 78)
225 g (8 oz) tomatoes, chopped
1 small green pepper, cored, seeded and diced
4 spring onions, chopped
8 black olives, stoned and chopped (optional)
1 tablespoon chopped fresh parsley, to garnish

Preparation time: 15 minutes
Cooking time: about 30 minutes

1. Place the lentils and chopped onion in a saucepan. Pour the water over and add the bay leaf and some salt. Bring to the boil, cover and simmer for about 30 minutes until the lentils are tender but not mushy.
2. Drain the lentils and place in a salad bowl. Stir in the French dressing while they are still warm and leave to cool. A
3. Stir in the tomatoes, green pepper, spring onions and black olives (if using).
4. Sprinkle with the chopped parsley and serve.
A Can be made up to 1 day ahead, covered and kept chilled.

FROM THE LEFT Lentil and tomato salad; Salami, haricot and tomato salad; Cracked wheat salad

1. Soak the haricot beans in the water overnight, or pour the same amount of boiling water over and soak for 2 hours.
2. Drain the beans, reserving the soaking water, and place in a saucepan. Make up the soaking water to 600 ml (1 pint) and add to the pan.
3. Skin and chop half the tomatoes and add to the beans in the pan. Add the sage and onion.
4. Bring to the boil, cover and simmer for 1-1½ hours until the beans are tender but not mushy. Drain, reserving 6 tablespoons of the cooking juice to use in the dressing.
5. For the dressing, mix the cooking juice with the wine vinegar, olive oil, salt and pepper and pour over the cooked beans. A
6. To serve, arrange overlapping slices of salami around the edge of a serving platter. Thinly slice the remaining tomatoes and arrange them inside the ring of salami slices. Pile the haricot bean salad in the centre of the platter and garnish with a sprig of fresh sage leaves.
A Can be made up to 1 day ahead, covered and kept chilled.

CRACKED WHEAT SALAD

Serves 8 as a starter or 6 as a side salad

225 g (8 oz) cracked wheat (burghul), soaked in
1 litre (1¾ pints) cold water for 1 hour
6 tablespoons olive oil
4 tablespoons lemon juice
6 tablespoons chopped fresh parsley
2 tablespoons chopped fresh mint or 1 tablespoon dried
mint
6 spring onions, thinly sliced
salt
freshly ground black pepper
To serve (optional):
1 lettuce
4 tomatoes, cut into wedges
1 × 5 cm (2 inch) piece cucumber, thickly sliced and
halved
8 black olives
sprigs of parsley or mint

**Preparation time: 10 minutes, plus soaking (plus
30 minutes if using dried mint)**

In the Lebanon, where this salad originates from, the preparation is highly individual and the quantities of ingredients vary with every family. If you like, quartered hard-boiled eggs can be included in the garnish.

1. Drain the cracked wheat in a sieve and squeeze out any excess water.
2. Pour the olive oil and lemon juice into a large mixing bowl. Add the parsley, mint, spring onions, salt and pepper, and mix well. (If using dried mint leave the mixture for 30 minutes.)
3. Add the drained cracked wheat to the dressing and mix thoroughly. A
4. To serve, arrange a bed of lettuce leaves on a serving plate or individual plates. Pile the salad into the centre and garnish the outside with tomato, cucumber, black olives and sprigs of parsley or mint. Alternatively the salad can simply be piled into a large serving bowl.
A Can be made up to 1 day in advance, covered and kept chilled.

SALADE DE CRUDITÉS

Serves 4 as a main salad or 6-8 as a starter
A selection of fresh young salad vegetables, e.g. 1 cos
    lettuce, ½ cucumber, 4 firm tomatoes, 1 bunch spring
    onions, 1 bunch radishes, 8 carrots, 100 g (4 oz)
    mushrooms, 1 bulb fennel, 1 red and 1 green pepper
Selection of dips:
150 ml (¼ pint) Mayonnaise (page 78)
150 ml (¼ pint) Hummus, see below
150 ml (¼ pint) Yogurt/soured cream dressing (page 79)

Preparation time: 10 minutes

1. Clean the vegetables well and arrange them in a
large shallow dish. Put the dips in small bowls.
2. Let everyone cut up their own vegetables which
are then dipped into the sauces.

HUMMUS

Serves 4 as a main salad or 6-8 as a starter
100 g (4 oz) chick peas
600 ml (1 pint) water
150 ml (¼ pint) plain unsweetened yogurt
2 tablespoons lemon juice
3 tablespoons tahini (sesame seed paste) or peanut butter
1 garlic clove, peeled and crushed
salt
freshly ground black pepper
paprika, to serve

Preparation time: 10 minutes, plus soaking
Cooking time: 1¼-1¾ hours

1. Soak the chick peas in the water overnight, or
alternatively soak in the same amount of boiling
water for 2 hours.
2. Pour the chick peas and soaking water into a
saucepan. Cover and boil for 10 minutes, then simmer for 1-1½ hours, adding more water if necessary, until the chick peas are soft enough to mash.
3. Drain the chick peas, reserving the cooking liquid.
4. Mash the chick peas with 2 tablespoons of the
cooking liquid. Beat in the yogurt, lemon juice,
tahini or peanut butter, garlic, and salt and pepper to
taste. Alternatively place all the ingredients in a
liquidizer and blend until smooth. Thin with a little
more of the cooking liquid if necessary. **A**
5. Serve sprinkled with paprika and accompanied
with warm pitta bread.
A Can be made up to 2 days in advance, covered and
chilled.

FROM THE RIGHT Hummus, Mayonnaise and Yogurt/soured cream dips

SPINACH AND SARDINE PÂTÉ

Serves 4 as a light main salad or 6-8 as a starter
500 g (1¼ lb) spinach
salt
15 g (½ oz) powdered gelatine
1 chicken stock cube
300 ml (½ pint) boiling water
1 × 100 g (4 oz) can sardines in oil
2 eggs, hard-boiled, shelled and chopped
150 ml (5 fl oz) soured cream
freshly ground black pepper

Preparation time: 15 minutes, plus cooling and setting
Cooking time: 10 minutes

This is an eye-catching and unusual way of presenting everyday ingredients. If you are using an intricate mould to set the pâté in the mixture will need to be fairly smooth to reproduce the pattern clearly.

1. Remove the coarse stalks from the spinach. Wash the leaves well. Place in a large saucepan with any water that clings to the leaves and a little salt. Cover and cook for 5-10 minutes, stirring occasionally, until the spinach wilts and is tender.
2. Drain the spinach, chop roughly and place in a mixing bowl.
3. Dissolve the gelatine and stock cube in the boiling water. Stir into the chopped spinach and leave until cool but not set.
4. Roughly chop the sardines in their oil and add with the chopped hard-boiled egg to the spinach mixture. Stir in the soured cream and add salt and pepper to taste.
5. Pour into a 1.2 litre (2 pint) soufflé dish, mould or 4-8 individual dishes. Chill in the refrigerator to set. A
6. To serve, either spoon from the dish or turn out on to a serving plate. Accompany with a mixed salad.
A Can be made up to 1 day ahead, covered and kept chilled.

EASTER EGG SALAD

Serves 4 as a main salad or 6-8 as a starter
skins from 2-3 large onions
6-8 eggs
1 lettuce, shredded
100 g (4 oz) bean-sprouts
300 ml (½ pint) Green mayonnaise (page 78), made using
    watercress
100 g (4 oz) lumpfish roe, to garnish (optional)

Preparation time: 15 minutes
Cooking time: 10 minutes

For a contrast, colour only half of the eggs and leave
the rest white.

1. Pour enough water into a saucepan to hard-boil
the eggs. Add the onion skins to the water and bring
to the boil. (The water will turn a deep golden
colour.)
2. Add the eggs to the pan and simmer for 8
minutes. Remove the eggs and plunge them into cold
water.
3. Shell the eggs and return them to the coloured
water. Simmer for 2 minutes until they are a rich
golden colour. Remove and leave to cool. [A]
4. To serve, arrange the shredded lettuce and bean-
sprouts on a large plate to resemble a bird's nest.
Place the hard-boiled eggs on top.
5. Pour some green mayonnaise over the eggs and
hand the rest separately in a jug. Garnish with
lumpfish roe, if liked.
[A] Can be prepared several hours in advance,
covered and kept chilled.

Why not try to sprout your own bean-sprouts? Any
dried beans that have not been split will sprout.
Soak 2 tablespoons in water overnight, then drain
them and put them in a clean jam jar. Fill the jar
with water and leave it in a dark place for 4 days
until the sprouts have grown. Rinse the beans and
change their water each day. The beans are easily
drained by covering the mouth of the jar with
muslin and pouring off the water.

CORONATION VEGETABLE SALAD

Serves 4-6 as a main salad
2 tablespoons oil
1 medium onion, peeled and thinly sliced
1 garlic clove, peeled and crushed (optional)
1 small cooking apple, peeled, cored and chopped
1 tablespoon curry powder
300 ml (½ pint) chicken stock
grated rind of ½ lemon
½ tablespoon lemon juice
225 g (8 oz) new potatoes, scrubbed or peeled
225 g (8 oz) new carrots, scrubbed or peeled
225 g (8 oz) cauliflower, divided into small florets
225 g (8 oz) small courgettes, cut into 5 mm (¼ inch)
    slices
50 g (2 oz) sultanas
To garnish:
25 g (1 oz) flaked almonds
1 tablespoon chopped fresh parsley

Preparation time: 20 minutes, plus cooling
Cooking time: 30 minutes

1. Heat the oil in a large saucepan and fry the onion,
garlic and apple for 5 minutes.
2. Stir in the curry powder and cook gently for 2
minutes. Stir in the stock, lemon rind and lemon
juice. Bring to the boil and simmer for 2 minutes.
3. Dice the potatoes and cut the carrots into 5 mm
(¼ inch) sticks. Add the potatoes and carrots to
the curry sauce, cover and simmer for 10 minutes.
4. Add the cauliflower florets, sliced courgettes and
sultanas to the pan, and stir gently. Cover and
simmer for about 10 minutes until the vegetables are
cooked but still crisp. Pour into a bowl and leave to
cool. [A]
5. To serve, toss the vegetables gently in their curry
sauce. Sprinkle with the flaked almonds and chopped parsley. Alternatively, the salad may be served
on a bed of lettuce or cold cooked rice.
[A] Can be made up to 1 day ahead, covered and kept
chilled.

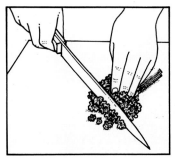

Holding the knife horizontally,
slice across the bunch of parsley
several times

Applying pressure to the tip, bring
the blade up and down until all
the parsley is finely chopped

FROM THE LEFT Spinach and sardine pâté; Easter egg salad; Coronation
vegetable salad

ALFALFA AND CRESS SALAD

Serves 4 as a main light salad
2 cartons mustard and cress
100 g (4 oz) alfalfa sprouts
225 g (8 oz) cooked ham, thinly sliced
4 eggs, hard-boiled, shelled and chopped
Yogurt-tartare dressing:
150 ml (5 fl oz) plain unsweetened yogurt
1 tablespoon capers
1 tablespoon chopped gherkins
1 tablespoon chopped stuffed olives
1 tablespoon chopped fresh parsley
salt
freshly ground black pepper
To garnish:
1 carton mustard and cress
50 g (2 oz) alfalfa sprouts (optional)

Preparation time: 15 minutes

1. Cut the mustard and cress from the carton, place in a mixing bowl and add the alfalfa sprouts.
2. Cut the ham into strips about 5 cm (2 inches) long and add to the salad with the chopped eggs. Toss to mix well.
3. Mix together all the dressing ingredients. Pour the dressing over the salad and toss until everything is evenly coated.
4. Pile the salad in the centre of a serving platter. Surround with a ring of mustard and cress or with little alternating piles of cress and alfalfa sprouts. Serve immediately, accompanied with warm crusty wholemeal bread. This salad is especially suitable for slimmers.

CHICORY AND ORANGE SALAD

Serves 4
3 large or 4 small heads chicory
3 medium oranges
1 shallot or small onion, peeled and cut in rings
4 tablespoons French dressing (page 78)
6 large or 8 small stuffed olives, to garnish

Preparation time: 15 minutes

1. Cut the chicory crosswise into slices and place in a salad bowl.
2. Cut away the peel and pith from the oranges. Cut the flesh into segments (see page 30) and add to the chicory, squeezing in any juice as well.
3. Pour the French dressing over and toss well.
4. Sprinkle the stuffed olives on top. A good accompaniment to salamis and cold meats.

DUCK, RED CABBAGE AND ROQUEFORT SALAD

Serves 4 as a light main salad or 6 as a starter
2 large portions duck breast, about 450 g (1 lb) each
2 tablespoons clear honey
225 g (8 oz) red cabbage
½ lettuce or endive
225 g (8 oz) Roquefort cheese
4 tablespoons French dressing (page 78)

Preparation time: 10 minutes
Cooking time: 15-20 minutes

1. Place the duck portions on a baking sheet and brush with the honey. Cook under a moderate grill for about 15 minutes, basting and turning until they are cooked through and the skin is crispy and well-browned. Leave to cool. [A]
2. Slice the red cabbage and lettuce very thinly and divide between 4 serving plates (or 6 plates if serving as a starter).
3. Thinly slice the duck breast and arrange on top of the shredded cabbage and lettuce.
4. Cut the Roquefort cheese into small cubes and sprinkle over the top of the salad.
5. Pour 1 tablespoon of French dressing over each salad plate just before serving.
[A] Can be made several hours in advance, covered and kept chilled.

Variation:
Substitute 4 small or 2 large chicken breasts for the duck and grill for a shorter time until cooked through.

This recipe is typical of the Nouvelle Cuisine style of cooking, where the emphasis is on luxurious ingredients, carefully but simply arranged. It is very important that all the components are of the best quality and in perfect condition, and that extra care is taken in arranging the food. To preserve the bright red colour of the cabbage it should be cut with a stainless steel knife. If you are preparing it in advance, toss it in French dressing or vinegar after shredding to prevent it turning blue. Roquefort is a very special cheese that has been produced since ancient times in the Massif Central region of France. Its unique and distinct flavour derives from the humid limestone caves in which it is matured. If you prefer a milder-flavoured cheese use Dolcelatte or blue Stilton. For a cheaper alternative try Danish blue.

FROM THE LEFT Chicory and orange salad; Alfalfa and cress salad; Duck, red cabbage and Roquefort salad

SLIMMERS' SPRING SALAD

Serves 4 as a light main salad or 6 as a starter

450 g (1 lb) cottage cheese
1 tablespoon chopped fresh parsley
1 tablespoon chopped fresh mint or 1 teaspoon dried mint
1 tablespoon chopped chives or spring onion tops, or
   1 teaspoon dried chives
4 large or 8 small black olives, stoned and chopped
salt
freshly ground black pepper
225 g (8 oz) ham, diced
1 × 225 g (8 oz) piece cucumber, diced
To serve:
1 lettuce or ½ large head endive
black olives
sprigs of mint or parsley

Preparation time: 15 minutes (plus 15 minutes if using dried herbs)

1. Put the cottage cheese in a mixing bowl. Stir in the parsley, mint, chives or spring onion tops, and black olives. Add salt and pepper to taste. If using dried herbs, leave the mixture for 15 minutes.
2. Add the diced ham and cucumber and stir into the cottage cheese mixture.
3. Serve at once or cover and chill until required. (Do not keep for too long, as the water will seep out of the cucumber and dilute the flavour.)
4. To serve, arrange the lettuce or endive leaves in a bowl or on a serving platter. Pile the cottage cheese salad in the centre and garnish with the olives and sprigs of mint or parsley.

Variation:
This salad is ideal as a starter to a rich main course. For special occasions it can be served in hollowed-out cucumber 'boats' or in avocado halves.

ARTICHOKES TARAMASALATA

Serves 4 as a starter or as a light main salad
4 globe artichokes
salt
Taramasalata:
100 g (4 oz) smoked cod's roe
150 ml (¼ pint) corn oil
150 ml (5 fl oz) plain unsweetened yogurt
2 tablespoons lemon juice
freshly ground black pepper
1 small garlic clove, peeled and crushed (optional)

Preparation time: 15 minutes, plus chilling
Cooking time: 20-40 minutes

1. Wash the artichokes and cut off the stalks. Cut across the tops and pull off any outer leaves that are dried or discoloured and, if preferred, shape the leaves by trimming about 2.5 cm (1 inch) off the points of the leaves, using scissors.
2. Cook the artichokes, uncovered, in a large pan of boiling salted water for about 20-40 minutes. The artichokes are ready when you can pull off a leaf easily, the time this takes will depend on the size and age of the artichokes. Remove from the pan and drain the artichokes upside down on a plate. [A]
3. For the taramasalata, peel off the skin from the cod's roe and place the roe in a mixing bowl (if the roe is difficult to peel, soak it in boiling water for a few seconds). Gradually, beat in the oil, yogurt and lemon juice until smooth. Add pepper and garlic to taste. Alternatively, put all the ingredients in a liquidizer and blend until smooth. Chill until required; this will thicken the sauce. [A] [F]
4. When the artichokes are cold remove the choke: spread the top leaves apart and pull out the central cone of soft small leaves. Scoop out the choke and discard, leaving the heart exposed.
5. Spoon the taramasalata into the centre of the artichokes. To eat, pull off an outside leaf and dip the fleshy base into the taramasalata.
[A] The artichokes and taramasalata may be made up to 1 day in advance. Keep separate, cover and chill.
[F] Thaw in the refrigerator for 8 hours or overnight, or for 4 hours at room temperature.

OPEN SALAD SANDWICH

Serves 4 as a light main salad or snack
4 large slices rye bread
175-225 g (6-8 oz) curd cheese
4 large crisp lettuce leaves
¼ small cucumber, thinly sliced
100 g (4 oz) smoked salmon, sliced
To garnish:
1 carton mustard and cress
lemon wedges

Preparation time: 10 minutes

1. Spread the slices of bread with the cheese.
2. Shred the lettuce and pile on top of the cheese.
3. Arrange the slices of cucumber and smoked salmon on the top in an attractive pattern. [A]
4. Place the open sandwiches on a platter and garnish with the mustard and cress and lemon wedges.
[A] Can be prepared several hours in advance, covered and kept chilled.

ARTICHOKE HEART SALAD

Serves 4 as a starter
4 medium-size cooked artichoke hearts
50 g (2 oz) button mushrooms, thinly sliced
4 tablespoons French dressing (page 78)
1 tablespoon chopped fresh parsley or chives
100 g (4 oz) streaky bacon, rinded

Preparation time: 10 minutes, plus standing

1. Put the artichoke hearts and mushrooms in a serving dish.
2. Mix the French dressing with the herbs and pour over. Toss well then leave to marinate for 10 minutes. [A]
3. Grill the bacon until crisp. Drain and leave to cool.
4. Just before serving, chop the bacon, add it to the salad and toss well.
[A] Can be made several hours in advance, covered and kept chilled.

Cutting across the top

Trimming the outer leaves

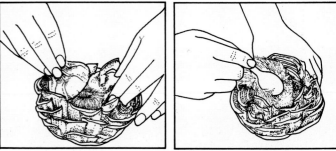

Removing the centre leaves   Spooning out the 'choke'

Artichokes taramasalata; Artichoke heart salad

ASPARAGUS MOUSSE SALAD

Serves 4 as a main salad or 6 as a starter
450 g (1 lb) fresh asparagus
300 ml (½ pint) water
25 g (1 oz) butter or margarine
25 g (1 oz) plain flour
15 g (½ oz) powdered gelatine, dissolved in 2 tablespoons hot water
150 ml (5 fl oz) soured cream or plain unsweetened yogurt
grated rind of ½ lemon
1 tablespoon lemon juice
1 egg, hard-boiled, shelled and finely chopped
salt
freshly ground black pepper
1 lettuce, to serve (optional)

Preparation time: 15 minutes, plus setting
Cooking time: 25-40 minutes

If fresh asparagus is not available, substitute 450 g (1 lb) frozen asparagus. Simmer the tips for 5 minutes, and the stems for 6-8 minutes, then use according to the recipe instructions.

1. Wash the asparagus and trim off any tough woody parts at the bottom of the stalks. Cut off the tips with about 5 cm (2 inches) of stem and simmer in the salted water for about 5-10 minutes until tender but not limp. Remove the tips with a slotted spoon and leave to cool.
2. Chop the remaining parts of the asparagus stems into small pieces and add to the simmering water. Cover and simmer for 15-30 minutes until soft. Drain, reserving the cooking water.
3. Make up the cooking water to 300 ml (½ pint) with water or milk. Melt the butter or margarine in a pan and stir in the flour. When smooth, gradually stir in the cooking liquid and bring to the boil, stirring until thickened. Add the drained chopped asparagus stems and simmer for 3 minutes, stirring from time to time.
4. Pour the sauce into a mixing bowl. Stir in the dissolved gelatine and leave until cool but not set.
5. Stir in the soured cream or yogurt, lemon rind and juice and chopped hard-boiled egg. Add salt and pepper to taste. Pour into a dish and chill until set. [A] Cover the reserved asparagus tips and chill until required.
6. To serve, arrange the lettuce leaves on individual plates. Place spoonfuls of mousse on top of the lettuce and garnish with the reserved asparagus tips. Alternatively, the mousse may be set in a 1.2 litre (2 pint) mould, turned out and garnished with lettuce leaves or asparagus tips.
[A] Can be made up to 1 day in advance, covered and kept chilled.

SPRING GREEN TERRINE

Serves 4 as a main salad or 8 as a starter
225 g (8 oz) streaky bacon, rinded
50 g (2 oz) butter or margarine
1 onion, peeled and chopped
1 garlic clove, peeled and crushed
350 g (12 oz) spring greens, coarse stalks removed
150 ml (¼ pint) water
salt
75 g (3 oz) breadcrumbs
2 eggs, beaten
grated nutmeg
freshly ground black pepper
2 eggs, hard-boiled, shelled
salad ingredients (e.g. endive, tomato), to garnish

Preparation time: 30 minutes
Cooking time: 40 minutes
Oven: 180°C, 350°F, Gas Mark 4

1. Stretch the bacon rashers with the blade of a blunt knife and lay them crosswise, overlapping, in a 450 g (1 lb) loaf tin, so that top and long sides are completely covered and at least 2.5 cm (1 inch) overlaps the sides of the tin.
2. Melt the butter in a large saucepan and fry the onion for 5 minutes, then add the garlic.
3. Wash the spring green leaves and shred them finely. Add to the pan with the water and some salt. Cover and cook for 10-15 minutes until tender. Drain and leave to cool.
4. Stir in the breadcrumbs and then the beaten eggs. Sprinkle with nutmeg, salt and pepper to taste.
5. Place half the greens mixture in the tin on top of the bacon. Lay the eggs down the centre and cover with the remaining greens mixture. Fold the overlapping bacon into the centre to enclose the filling.
6. Cover the tin with foil and bake in a preheated oven for 40 minutes until firm. Leave to cool. [A]
7. Turn out on to a serving dish and garnish with salad ingredients. Cut into 8 slices.
[A] Can be made up to 1 day ahead, covered and kept chilled.

Variation:
At a time of year when the range of vegetables available is rather uninspiring, this makes an unusual salad dish. To convert it into a vegetarian salad, line the loaf tin with rinsed, preserved vine leaves rather than bacon rashers. Spring Green Terrine is portable enough to take on a summer picnic; if spring greens are no longer available use young spinach leaves instead.

FROM THE LEFT Asparagus mousse salad; Spring green terrine

WILTED SPINACH SALAD

Serves 4 as a side salad or 6-8 as a starter

225 g (8 oz) young, fresh spinach leaves
2 tablespoons oil
100 g (4 oz) streaky bacon, rinded and chopped
1 small garlic clove, peeled and crushed (optional)
1 tablespoon lemon juice

Preparation time: 5 minutes
Cooking time: 5 minutes

1. Wash the spinach thoroughly and remove the coarse stalks. Drain and dry the leaves. Leave the smaller leaves whole and shred the larger ones. Put all the spinach in a large bowl.

2. For the dressing, heat the oil in a small saucepan and add the chopped bacon and garlic. Fry for 5 minutes until the bacon is browned and crisp, moving the pieces around the pan to prevent them from sticking together.

3. Remove from the heat and immediately pour in the lemon juice (take care as it will splutter). Stir quickly and pour over the spinach immediately, while the dressing is still hot. Toss well until all the leaves are coated and have begun to wilt. **A** This salad goes particularly well with grilled or fried meats such as veal escalopes, chops or sausages.

A Can be made several hours in advance, covered and kept chilled.

SUMMER

CHICKEN, TARRAGON AND ORANGE SALAD

Serves 4 as a main salad
1 chicken, about 1½ kg (3 lb), with giblets
1 medium onion, peeled and thinly sliced
grated rind and juice of 1 orange
1 tablespoon chopped fresh tarragon, or ½ tablespoon
   dried tarragon
1 bay leaf
300 ml (½ pint) water
salt
freshly ground black pepper
1 tablespoon olive or salad oil
½-1 tablespoon wine vinegar
To garnish:
1 small orange, peeled and sliced
1 carton mustard and cress
fresh tarragon sprigs, if available

Preparation time: 20 minutes
Cooking time: 45 minutes-1 hour

1. Choose a large saucepan and put in it the chicken giblets, sliced onion, orange rind and juice, tarragon and bay leaf.
2. Put the chicken in the saucepan, pour the water over and sprinkle with salt and pepper. Cover, bring to the boil and simmer for 45 minutes-1 hour, basting several times, until the chicken is cooked.
3. Lift out the chicken and leave to cool. Discard the bay leaf, giblets and onion. Measure the stock.
4. Boil the stock to reduce to 300 ml (½ pint). Leave to cool, then chill in the refrigerator. [F]
5. When the chicken is cold, take the meat off the bones, discarding the skin (the bones may be used for making stock). [F] [A] Cut the meat into bite-size pieces and place in a mixing bowl.
6. When the stock is chilled, remove the layer of fat from the top. Reheat the stock gently to thin it, stir in the oil, and add vinegar, salt and pepper to taste. Pour this dressing over the chicken and toss well.
7. Serve at once or cover and chill until required. To serve, turn into a serving dish and garnish with orange slices, cress and tarragon sprigs. The salad may also be served on a bed of lettuce.
[F] Freeze stock and chicken meat separately. Thaw for 8 hours or overnight in the refrigerator.
[A] Can be prepared up to 1 day in advance, covered and kept chilled.

LETTUCE AND ORANGE SALAD WITH BUTTER AND ALMOND DRESSING

Serves 4-6 as a side salad
1 Webb's Wonderful or other crisp lettuce
2 oranges
100 g (4 oz) butter
50 g (2 oz) blanched almonds, cut into slivers
1 tablespoon lemon juice
salt
freshly ground black pepper

Preparation time: 10 minutes
Cooking time: 5 minutes

1. Tear the lettuce into pieces and place in a salad bowl.
2. Remove the peel and pith from the oranges and cut the flesh into segments between the membranes. Add the orange segments to the lettuce and squeeze any orange juice over the top.
3. Melt the butter in a saucepan. Fry the almonds, stirring constantly, until golden brown; about 3 minutes.
4. Allow the almonds to cool slightly, then stir the lemon juice, salt and pepper into the pan.
5. Pour the still warm dressing over the lettuce and the orange segments and toss until well coated.
6. Serve as a side salad. This is particularly good with chicken and fish dishes.

To obtain neat orange segments without any pith on them, cut a slice off the top and bottom of an orange and stand it on a board. With a small serrated knife make smooth downward cuts, following the curve of the orange. When you have been around the orange once, repeat the process to check that all the pith has been removed. To cut the segments hold the orange gently but firmly in the palm of one hand and, with a sharp paring knife, cut down on either side of each membrane into the centre of the orange, freeing and removing one segment at a time.

FROM THE TOP Lettuce and orange salad with butter and almond dressing;
Chicken, tarragon and orange salad

CAESAR SALAD

Serves 4-6 as a side salad or starter
2 tablespoons corn or olive oil
1 garlic clove, peeled and crushed
2 thick slices bread, trimmed and cut into 1 cm (½ inch)
   cubes
1 cos lettuce
1 × 50 g (2 oz) can anchovy fillets
25 g (1 oz) grated Parmesan cheese
3 tablespoons olive oil
1 tablespoon lemon juice
salt
freshly ground black pepper
1 egg

Preparation time: 15 minutes
Cooking time: 2 minutes

1. Heat the oil in a frying pan and add the garlic. Fry the bread cubes until crisp and golden brown all over. Drain.
2. Tear or cut the lettuce into bite-size pieces and place in a salad bowl.
3. Chop the anchovy fillets and add to the lettuce with the oil from the anchovy can and the Parmesan cheese.
4. Add the olive oil, lemon juice, salt and pepper and toss well.
5. Cook the egg in a pan of boiling water for 1 minute. Break the egg over the salad and toss gently. Add the croûtons, toss again and serve.

ITALIAN TOMATO SALAD

Serves 4 as a side salad or 6 as a starter
6 tomatoes, weighing together about 750 g (1½ lb), thinly
   sliced
175 g (6 oz) Mozzarella cheese, thinly sliced
10-12 small black olives
Dressing:
4 tablespoons olive oil
1½ tablespoons wine vinegar
2 tablespoons chopped fresh basil or 2 teaspoons dried
   basil
salt
freshly ground black pepper

Preparation time: 10 minutes (plus 15 minutes if using dried basil)

1. Arrange the sliced tomatoes over the base of a shallow serving dish.
2. Place the Mozzarella slices in the centre, on top of the tomatoes, so that the tomatoes are visible around the edge of the dish.
3. Arrange the black olives on top.
4. For the dressing, mix the oil with the vinegar, basil, salt and pepper (leave to marinate for at least 15 minutes if the basil is dried).
5. Pour the dressing over the tomatoes, cheese and olives. A As a side salad this goes particularly well with salamis, fried chicken, or veal.
A Can be prepared several hours in advance, covered and kept chilled.

PIPÉRADE TOMATOES

Serves 4 as a starter or as a light main course
4 large tomatoes, preferably Mediterranean
50 g (2 oz) butter
2 rashers streaky bacon, rinded and chopped
1 shallot, peeled and finely chopped
1 small red or green pepper, cored, seeded and diced
4 eggs, lightly beaten
salt
freshly ground black pepper
1 small lettuce, to serve

Preparation time: 10 minutes
Cooking time: 20 minutes

1. Slice the tops off the tomatoes, and reserve as lids.
2. Scoop out the insides of the tomatoes (a grapefruit knife makes this very easy) and chop up the flesh.
3. Melt 25 g (1 oz) butter in a saucepan, and fry the bacon, shallot and pepper for 5 minutes.
4. Add the tomato flesh and simmer for 10 minutes, stirring occasionally, until reduced to a thick purée.
5. In another saucepan melt the remaining butter and pour in the beaten eggs. Cook gently, stirring with a wooden spoon, until the eggs are scrambled.
6. Stir the pipérade mixture into the scrambled eggs and add salt and pepper to taste. Leave to cool.
7. Fill the tomato cases with the cold pipérade and replace the lids. Serve on a bed of lettuce.

GREEK SALAD WITH TAHINI DRESSING

Serves 4-6 as a side salad
½ large cucumber, about 350 g (12 oz)
350 g (12 oz) tomatoes, cut into thin wedges
1 small green pepper, quartered, seeded and sliced
1 small onion, peeled and thinly sliced
8 small black olives, stoned and halved
100 g (4 oz) feta cheese (optional)
Tahini dressing:
2 tablespoons tahini paste
4 tablespoons plain unsweetened yogurt
1-2 tablespoons water
2 tablespoons chopped fresh parsley
1 small garlic clove, crushed (optional)
salt
freshly ground black pepper

Preparation time: 15 minutes

1. Cut the cucumber into 5 mm (¼ inch) slices, then cut these across into 5 mm (¼ inch) batons and place in a salad bowl.
2. Add the tomatoes, green pepper, onions and olives.
3. For the dressing, spoon the tahini paste into a small bowl. Slowly beat in the yogurt and thin down with the water as necessary. Stir in the parsley and garlic, and salt and pepper to taste.
4. Pour the dressing over the salad and toss well. Cube the feta cheese and sprinkle over.
6. Goes well with cold roast meats and pitta bread.

MEDITERRANEAN BEAN SALAD

Serves 4 as a side salad or 6 as a starter
450 g (1 lb) green beans (French or runner)
salt
6 tablespoons olive oil
grated rind of 1 small lemon
2 tablespoons lemon juice
1 small garlic clove, peeled and crushed (optional)
2 eggs, hard-boiled, shelled and finely chopped
8 small black olives
freshly ground black pepper

Preparation time: 10 minutes
Cooking time: 5 minutes

1. If using French beans, top and tail them. If they are small, leave them whole; halve them if large. String runner beans and slice diagonally.
2. Put the prepared beans into a saucepan with a little salt. Pour over just enough boiling water to cover and simmer for about 5 minutes until just cooked, but not limp and soft.
3. Drain the beans and rinse under cold water to cool quickly.
4. For the dressing, pour the olive oil into a bowl large enough to hold the beans. Add the lemon rind, lemon juice, garlic, chopped eggs, olives, salt and pepper and mix well.
5. Add the cooled beans to the dressing and toss until well coated. [A] As a side salad this goes well with cold chicken, meat or fish.
[A] Can be made several hours in advance, covered and kept chilled.

Variation:
For a stronger Mediterranean flavour add a 50 g (2 oz) can of anchovy fillets, sliced, with the cooled beans.

BROAD BEAN AND BACON SALAD

Serves 4-6 as a side salad
450 g (1 lb) shelled broad beans
salt
2 tablespoons chopped fresh parsley
150 ml (5 fl oz) plain unsweetened yogurt
freshly ground black pepper
4 rashers streaky bacon, rinded, to garnish

Preparation time: 10 minutes
Cooking time: 5-10 minutes

PASTA PISTOU SALAD

Serves 4 as a side salad or 6 as a starter
225 g (8 oz) pasta (spaghetti, noodles, shell shapes, etc)
25 g (1 oz) fresh basil leaves (about 4 large sprigs), chopped
25 g (1 oz) grated Parmesan cheese
1 garlic clove, peeled and crushed
6 tablespoons olive oil
1 tablespoon lemon juice
salt
freshly ground black pepper
25 g (1 oz) pine kernels or chopped flaked almonds

Preparation time: 5 minutes
Cooking time: 15 minutes

If fresh basil is not available substitute 2 tablespoons chopped fresh parsley and 1 tablespoon dried basil, or use 2-3 tablespoons ready-made pistou sauce from a jar.

1. Cook the pasta in a large pan of boiling salted water for 10-15 minutes until cooked 'al dente', or according to the pack instructions.
2. Drain and rinse under cold water to cool quickly.
3. For the dressing, place the basil in a mixing bowl large enough to hold the pasta. Add the Parmesan, garlic, oil, lemon juice, salt and pepper. Beat until well mixed. Alternatively place all the dressing ingredients in a liquidizer and blend until smooth.
4. Stir in the pine kernels or chopped almonds, then add the cold pasta and toss well until it is all thoroughly coated. If the pasta absorbs a lot of oil, add another 1-2 tablespoons. [A] This salad is ideal to serve with ham and other cold meats, salamis, and tomatoes in French dressing (page 78).
[A] Can be prepared up to 1 day ahead, covered and kept chilled.

1. Put the broad beans in a saucepan and add a little salt. Pour over just enough boiling water to cover and simmer for about 5 minutes until tender. Drain and rinse under cold water to cool quickly.
2. Grill the bacon until crispy. Drain and cool.
3. For the dressing, stir the chopped parsley into the yogurt and add salt and pepper to taste.
4. Stir the dressing into the cooled beans. Turn the bean salad into a serving dish and crumble the crispy bacon over the top. [A] As a side salad this is an especially good accompaniment to cold roast lamb.
[A] Can be made several hours in advance, covered and kept chilled.

CLOCKWISE FROM TOP Pasta pistou salad; Broad bean and bacon salad; Mediterranean bean salad

SALAD SALMON STEAKS

Serves 4 as a main salad
4 salmon steaks, about 175 g (6 oz) each
salt
freshly ground black pepper
1 lemon
4 sprigs parsley or dill
4 tablespoons dry white wine or water
1 small cucumber, about 25 cm (10 inches) long
about 150 ml (¼ pint) Mayonnaise (page 78)
To serve:
1 lettuce
sprigs of dill or parsley

Preparation time: 15 minutes
Cooking time: 20 minutes
Oven: 180°C, 350°F, Gas Mark 4

1. Put the salmon steaks in a greased ovenproof dish and sprinkle with salt and pepper.
2. Grate the rind from the lemon and reserve for the sauce. Cut the lemon into thin slices and place one slice on top of each steak.
3. Place a sprig of parsley or dill on top of each salmon steak and pour the wine or water over.
4. Cover the dish with foil and bake in a preheated oven for about 20 minutes until the salmon is cooked but not dry. Leave to cool. [A]
5. For the sauce, cut the cucumber into 5 mm (¼ inch) slices, and then into small dice. Place in a mixing bowl.
6. Stir the mayonnaise into the cucumber with any salmon cooking liquid, the reserved lemon rind, salt and pepper. Add a little more mayonnaise if you want a larger quantity of sauce.
7. To serve, carefully remove the skin (if preferred) and the central bone from the salmon, keeping the steaks whole. Discard the lemon slice and parsley or dill. Arrange the steaks on a serving plate. Spoon cucumber sauce down the centre of each salmon steak where the bone has been removed. Select the crispest leaves from the lettuce heart and use as a garnish and place a sprig of dill or parsley on top of each steak.
[A] The salmon steaks and the poaching liquid can be covered and kept separately in the refrigerator for 1 day.

Variation:
Halibut, turbot – even cod – can be used for this recipe instead of salmon. If dill is hard to find, use the feathery leaves from the top of fennel bulbs instead.

SEAFOOD STUFFED LETTUCE

Serves 4 as a main salad or 6-8 as a starter
1 large, round lettuce
4 eggs, hard-boiled, shelled and chopped
225 g (8 oz) shelled prawns
175 g (6 oz) crabmeat, fresh, frozen or canned
150 ml (¼ pint) Anchovy mayonnaise (page 78)
1 tablespoon lemon juice
2 tablespoons chopped fresh chives
2 tablespoons chopped fresh parsley
salt
freshly ground black pepper
8 unshelled prawns, to garnish (optional)

Preparation time: 15 minutes

1. Remove and discard the ragged outside leaves from the lettuce, but keep the rest whole. Carefully wash the lettuce and shake to remove excess water. Leave to drain upside down on paper towels or a clean teatowel.
2. For the stuffing, place the chopped eggs in a mixing bowl and add the shelled prawns and crabmeat. Stir in the anchovy mayonnaise, lemon juice, chives and parsley. Add plenty of salt and pepper. [A]
3. Place the lettuce on a large plate. Gently pull apart the leaves to make a hole in the centre. Pluck out the lettuce heart.
4. Spoon the stuffing into the centre of the lettuce. Garnish with unshelled prawns.
[A] The stuffing can be made several hours in advance, covered and kept chilled.

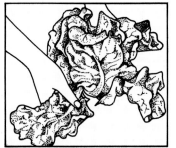
Removing ragged leaves

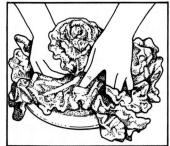
Plucking out the heart

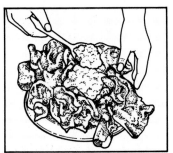
Spooning in the filling

AUBERGINE SALAD

Serves 4 as a side salad

500 g (1¼ lb) aubergine
1 tablespoon salt
5 tablespoons olive oil
1 medium onion, peeled and chopped
1 garlic clove, peeled and crushed
2 large tomatoes
50 g (2 oz) chopped walnuts
1 tablespoon chopped fresh oregano or basil or 1 teaspoon
    dried oregano or basil
150 ml (¼ pint) Yogurt/soured cream dressing (page 79)
salt
freshly ground black pepper
1 tablespoon chopped fresh parsley, to garnish

Preparation time: 15 minutes, plus draining
Cooking time: 10 minutes

1. Cut the aubergine into 1 cm (½ inch) dice and place in a colander. Sprinkle with the salt, shake to mix and leave to drain for about 1 hour over a plate until the bitter juices have run out. Rinse in water and drain well.

2. Heat the oil in a large frying pan and add the diced aubergine in one layer. Add the onion and garlic. Cook over a moderate heat for 10 minutes, stirring frequently, until the aubergine is tender and browned all over. Leave to cool.

3. Place the fried aubergine in a mixing bowl. Cut the tomatoes into similar sized dice and add to the aubergine with the walnuts. Ⓐ

4. Stir the herbs into the yogurt dressing and add salt and pepper to taste. Pour the dressing over the salad and mix well.

5. Transfer the salad to a serving bowl and sprinkle with the chopped parsley. Cover and chill until required. Delicious with cold roast meats.

Ⓐ Can be made several hours in advance, covered and kept chilled.

Salad salmon steaks; Seafood stuffed lettuce

MIDSUMMER SALAD

Serves 4 as a side salad or starter
1 small ripe melon
100 g (4 oz) strawberries, hulled
1 × 7.5 cm (3 inch) piece cucumber
1 small crisp lettuce, shredded
4 tablespoons French dressing (page 78)
2 tablespoons chopped fresh mint
salt
freshly ground black pepper
15 g (½ oz) flaked almonds, to garnish

Preparation time: 15 minutes

1. Cut the melon into quarters, then remove the seeds and skin. Cut the flesh into cubes, about 1 cm (½ inch) square, or scoop into balls.
2. Cut the strawberries and cucumber into thin slices.
3. To serve, arrange the shredded lettuce on a large serving dish or 4 individual plates. Arrange the pieces of melon, strawberry and cucumber on top of the lettuce.
4. Mix the French dressing with the chopped mint and add salt and pepper. Pour over the salad just before serving, and sprinkle with the almonds. As a side salad this goes very well with a selection of hard and soft cheeses, or ham.

Variations:
Use small ogen melons, allowing half a melon per person. Arrange the salad in the scooped out melon halves rather than on plates. Substitute sliced banana or kiwi fruit for some or all of the strawberries.

PEPERONATA

Serves 4 as a side salad or 6-8 as a starter
2 tablespoons olive oil
1 large onion, peeled and sliced
500 g (1¼ lb) red and green peppers, quartered and seeded
1 garlic clove, peeled and crushed (optional)
500 g (1¼ lb) tomatoes, skinned
salt
freshly ground black pepper

**Preparation time: 10 minutes, plus cooling
Cooking time: 40-50 minutes**

BOTTOM Courgette timbale salad; TOP Midsummer Salad with (FROM THE TOP) Walnut Crediou, Mélusine, Brie, Munster and Emmental cheeses

COURGETTE TIMBALE SALAD

Serves 4 as a light main salad or 8 as a starter
750 g (1½ lb) courgettes, sliced
salt
1 tablespoon chopped fresh basil or mint
4 eggs, beaten
150 ml (5 fl oz) single cream or milk
freshly ground black pepper
2 tablespoons grated Parmesan cheese
To serve:
4 tomatoes, thinly sliced
1 carton mustard and cress
2-3 tablespoons French dressing (page 78)

**Preparation time: 15 minutes
Cooking time: 50 minutes (35 minutes if cooking as a starter in smaller moulds)
Oven: 180°C, 350°F, Gas Mark 4**

1. Cook the courgettes in boiling water for 5 minutes.
2. Drain, add the chopped herbs and purée in a liquidizer, food processor or mouli-légumes.
3. Stir the beaten eggs into the courgette purée with the cream or milk. Add plenty of salt and pepper.
4. Pour into 4 well-greased 300 ml (½ pint) ramekins. Sprinkle each with Parmesan and bake in a preheated oven for about 45 minutes until set. (For a starter bake in 8 × 150 ml (¼ pint) ramekins for 20-30 minutes.) Leave to cool, then chill. [A]
5. Turn the timbales out on to individual plates. Surround with the tomato slices and the mustard and cress. Spoon the French dressing over.
[A] Can be made up to 1 day in advance, covered and kept chilled.

1. Heat the oil in a large pan and fry the onion for 5 minutes.
2. Cut the peppers into slices about 5 mm (¼ inch) thick and add to the pan with the garlic. Stir together and cover the pan. Simmer for 15 minutes until the peppers are tender but not too soft.
3. Cut each tomato into 8 wedges and add to the peppers with salt and pepper.
4. Simmer uncovered, stirring occasionally, for 15-20 minutes until tender. (The tomatoes will cook down but will still be just recognizable as wedges.)
5. Turn the vegetables and their juice into a serving bowl and leave to cool. Taste and add more seasoning if necessary. [F] [A] Served as a side salad, this is particularly good with cold roast meats.
[F] Thaw for 8 hours or overnight in the refrigerator, or for 4 hours at room temperature.
[A] Can be made up to 1 day in advance, covered and kept chilled.

FRENCH LAMB SALAD

Serves 4 as a light main salad
450 g (1 lb) cold roast lamb (preferably cooked slightly rare)
4 tablespoons olive or salad oil
2 tablespoons wine vinegar
2 tablespoons concentrated mint sauce or 2 tablespoons chopped fresh mint
salt
freshly ground black pepper
4 spring onions, chopped
225 g (8 oz) cooked peas
To serve:
1 lettuce
sprigs of mint

Preparation time: 10 minutes

1. Cut the lamb into 2 cm (¾ inch) cubes.
2. For the dressing, pour the oil into a bowl large enough to hold the meat and vegetables. Add the vinegar, mint sauce or fresh mint, salt and pepper and mix well.
3. Add the chopped spring onions and the cubes of meat and toss until well coated. Gently stir in the peas. [A]
4. Just before serving, shred the lettuce and stir into the lamb salad. Turn on to a serving dish and garnish with sprigs of mint.
[A] May be made several hours in advance, covered and kept chilled.

BEETROOT AND ORANGE SALAD

Serves 4 as a side salad
450 g (1 lb) cooked beetroot, skinned
150 ml (5 fl oz) soured cream
1 medium orange
2 tablespoons chopped fresh chives
salt
freshly ground black pepper

Preparation time: 10 minutes

1. Cut the beetroot into dice about 1 cm (½ inch) square and arrange in a shallow serving dish.
2. Put the soured cream into a mixing bowl. Add the grated rind and juice from half the orange. Cut the peel and pith away from the remaining orange half and cut the flesh into segments (see page 30).
3. Scatter the orange segments over the beetroot.
4. Mix the chives, salt and pepper with the soured cream. Pour this dressing over the beetroot and orange, but do not stir. Serve at once.

MARINATED MACKEREL

Serves 4 as a main salad
4 medium mackerel, heads removed, gutted and cleaned
150 ml (¼ pint) dry cider
150 ml (¼ pint) water
1 slice lemon
large sprig of parsley
large sprig of thyme
1 bay leaf
salt
freshly ground black pepper
To garnish:
1 tablespoon chopped fresh parsley
1 tablespoon chopped fresh chives
shredded lettuce or sliced cucumber

Preparation time: 10 minutes, plus cooling and marinating
Cooking time: 30 minutes
Oven: 180°C, 350°F, Gas Mark 4

1. Place the prepared mackerel in an ovenproof dish or roasting tin. Pour over the cider and water and add the lemon, herbs, salt and pepper.
2. Cover and bake for 20-30 minutes until tender.
3. Remove the fish, cool, then remove the skin.
4. Pour the cooking liquid into a saucepan and boil to reduce to about 150 ml (¼ pint).
5. Place the mackerel in a shallow serving dish and pour over the reduced liquid. Cover and leave to marinate in a cool place. [A]
6. To serve, sprinkle with the chopped parsley and chives, and garnish with lettuce or cucumber.
[A] Can be made up to 1 day in advance, covered and kept chilled.

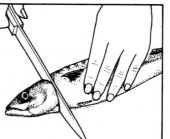
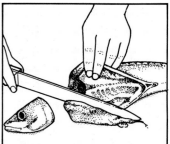
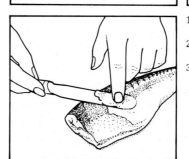

1. Cutting off the head
2. Removing the guts
3. Peeling the skin off the cooked fish with a palette knife

COURGETTE RATATOUILLE

Serves 4 as a side salad or 6-8 as a starter

2 tablespoons olive oil
1 medium onion, peeled and thinly sliced
1 garlic clove, peeled and crushed
450 g (1 lb) courgettes, sliced
225 g (8 oz) tomatoes, skinned and sliced
1 small aubergine, diced
1 green pepper, quartered, seeded and sliced crosswise
    into thin strips
1 tablespoon chopped fresh oregano or 1 teaspoon dried
    oregano
salt
freshly ground black pepper
1 tablespoon chopped fresh parsley, to garnish

Preparation time: 15 minutes
Cooking time: 35 minutes

This dish originates from Provence in Southern France. It is good hot or cold, and is almost better if kept for a day before serving.

1. Heat the oil in a large saucepan and fry the onion and garlic for 5 minutes.
2. Add the courgettes, tomatoes, aubergine and green pepper to the pan. Sprinkle with the oregano, salt and pepper and stir gently.
3. Bring to the boil, stirring gently. Cover and simmer for about 30 minutes until the vegetables are tender but not too soft. Leave to cool. [F] [A]
4. To serve, turn into a serving dish and sprinkle with the chopped parsley. As a side salad this makes a good accompaniment to grilled meats.
[F] Thaw in the refrigerator for 8 hours or overnight, or at room temperature for 4 hours.
[A] Can be made up to 1 day in advance, covered and kept chilled.

Beetroot and orange salad; Marinated mackerel

SEAFOOD MOUSSE

Serves 4 as a main salad or 6-8 as a starter
450 g (1 lb) salmon trout or 350 g (12 oz) middle cut of
   salmon
150 ml (¼ pint) dry white wine
150 ml (¼ pint) water
1 small onion, peeled and sliced
1 slice lemon
sprigs of parsley and thyme
1 bay leaf
salt
black peppercorns
Sauce:
25 g (1 oz) butter or margarine
25 g (1 oz) plain flour
300 ml (½ pint) cooking liquid
1 teaspoon lemon juice
1 teaspoon anchovy essence
1 egg, separated
150 ml (5 fl oz) plain unsweetened yogurt or soured cream
freshly ground black pepper
15 g (½ oz) powdered gelatine
To garnish:
green salad vegetables (cucumber, watercress)
Green mayonnaise (page 78)

**Preparation time: 20 minutes, plus cooling and
setting
Cooking time: 20 minutes
Oven: 180°C, 350°F, Gas Mark 4**

1. Clean the fish and place in an ovenproof dish.
2. Pour the wine and water into a saucepan and add
the flavourings. Bring to the boil and pour over the
fish. Cover and bake in a preheated oven for 15-20
minutes until just cooked. Leave to cool.
3. Drain off the cooking liquid and make up to
300 ml (½ pint) with milk. Remove the head, tail,
skin and bones from the fish, and flake the flesh.
4. For the sauce, melt the butter in a saucepan and
stir in the flour. When blended, stir in the reserved
cooking liquid and bring to the boil, stirring until
thickened. Simmer for 2 minutes, stirring occasionally.
5. Place the flaked fish in a mixing bowl and stir the
sauce in. Mix in the lemon juice, anchovy essence,
egg yolk, and yogurt or soured cream. Add salt and
pepper to taste.
6. Dissolve the gelatine in 2 tablespoons of hot water
and stir into the mousse. Whisk the egg white until
stiff and fold in. Turn into a 900 ml (1½ pint) mould
and chill until set. A
7. To serve, turn out on to a plate and garnish with
salad vegetables. Serve with green mayonnaise. A
A The mousse can be made up to 1 day in advance,
covered and kept chilled. The mayonnaise can be
made 2 days in advance, covered and kept chilled.

PICKLED CUCUMBER SALAD WITH DILL

Serves 4-6 as a side salad
1 large cucumber
1 tablespoon salt
Dressing:
4 tablespoons wine vinegar
1 tablespoon caster sugar
1 tablespoon chopped fresh dill or 1 teaspoon dried dill
freshly ground black pepper
1 tablespoon chopped fresh dill or parsley, to garnish

Preparation time: 10 minutes, plus draining and chilling

1. Score the skin of the cucumber by running the prongs of a fork down its length, all the way round.
2. Slice the cucumber as thinly as possible so that the slices are transparent (this is most easily done with a mandoline).
3. Place the cucumber slices in a colander or sieve and sprinkle with the salt. Shake to distribute the salt over all the slices and place the colander over a bowl to drain.
4. Leave at room temperature for 1-2 hours, shaking occasionally, until about 100 ml (3½ fl oz) juice has drained off.
5. Rinse the cucumber in cold water to remove excess salt and drain well (the slices should be very limp). Place in a shallow serving dish.
6. Mix all the dressing ingredients together and pour over the cucumber slices. Chill well. Ⓐ
7. Serve sprinkled with the chopped dill or parsley. This side salad is particularly good with cold salmon and other fish dishes.
Ⓐ Can be prepared up to 1 day in advance, covered and kept chilled.

Variation:
Because this refreshing Scandinavian salad is best made a day in advance, it is a very good choice for a summer buffet party, especially one which has salmon on the menu. Tzatziki, an equally refreshing Greek salad, is made in a similar way but uses fresh cucumber and a combination of fresh mint and yogurt instead of a dill dressing.

ORIENTAL MANGETOUT SALAD

Serves 4 as a light main salad or 6-8 as a starter
500 g (1¼ lb) mangetout peas
salt
100 g (4 oz) button mushrooms, thinly sliced
1 small red pepper, cored, seeded and finely chopped
225 g (8 oz) peeled prawns
2 tablespoons sesame seeds, to garnish
Dressing:
3 tablespoons oil (sunflower, safflower, sesame seed or
    corn oil)
1 tablespoon soy sauce
1-2 tablespoons lemon juice
1 teaspoon brown or white sugar (optional)

Preparation time: 10-15 minutes
Cooking time: 1 minute

1. Top and tail the mangetout and string them if necessary. Plunge into a pan of boiling salted water, return to the boil and simmer for 1 minute. Drain immediately and rinse under cold water to cool quickly. Drain again and leave to cool.
2. Combine the dressing ingredients in a large mixing bowl, adding lemon juice to taste and sugar if a sweet dressing is preferred.
3. Toss the mushrooms in the dressing until thoroughly coated. Add the red pepper.
4. Add the drained mangetout and the prawns and toss well to make sure that everything is coated in dressing. Ⓐ
5. To serve, turn into one large or several small bowls and sprinkle with the sesame seeds.
Ⓐ Can be made up to 1 day in advance, covered and kept chilled.

Variation:
If you are lucky enough to find sugar peas, they can be used instead of mangetout for this salad. Sugar peas look rather like swollen mangetout and require no cooking at all as they are extremely tender and deliciously sweet (tasting literally of sugar).

FROM THE TOP Oriental mangetout salad; Country salad

GRATED COURGETTE AND MINT SALAD

Serves 4 as a side salad
750 g (1½ lb) courgettes
2 teaspoons salt
50 g (2 oz) pine kernels or flaked almonds
100 g (4 oz) sultanas
Dressing:
6 tablespoons olive oil
2 tablespoons lemon juice
2 tablespoons chopped fresh mint
freshly ground black pepper

Preparation time: 10 minutes, plus draining

1. Wash the courgettes and grate coarsely into a colander or sieve. Sprinkle the salt over, shake to distribute the salt evenly and place the colander over a bowl to drain. Leave for about 1 hour until the juices have run out. Rinse off the excess salt, drain and pat dry.
2. Place the grated courgettes in a mixing bowl and add the pine kernels or flaked almonds and sultanas.
3. Mix together all the dressing ingredients and pour over the courgette salad. Toss to mix well.
4. Serve as a side salad with cold meats (particularly cold roast lamb or chicken).

COUNTRY SALAD

Serves 4 as a side salad
1 small lettuce
1 bunch dandelion leaves
100 g (4 oz) corn salad or purslane
1 small bunch sorrel
1 small bunch chives
150 ml (¼ pint) Soured cream blue cheese dressing
  (page 79)

Preparation time: 10 minutes

1. Wash the lettuce, shred coarsely and place in a salad bowl.
2. Wash the dandelion leaves, removing the coarse stalks, and add to the lettuce.
3. Wash the corn salad or purslane, separate into sprigs and add to the salad.
4. Finely shred the sorrel and chop the chives. Add both to the salad.
5. Pour the blue cheese dressing over and toss well. Serve.

AUTUMN

MELON AND PARMA HAM SALAD WITH GINGER DRESSING

Serves 4 as a starter
1 medium honeydew melon, weighing about 1 kg (2 lb)
100 g (4 oz) thinly sliced Parma ham
Ginger dressing:
25 g (1 oz) stem ginger
2 tablespoons stem ginger syrup
3 tablespoons salad oil
1 teaspoon lemon juice
freshly ground black pepper

Preparation time: 10 minutes

1. Cut the melon into quarters lengthways. Discard the seeds and cut off the skin. Cut each melon quarter into 4 long slices, making 16 slices altogether.
2. Cut the Parma ham into long slices about 5 cm (2 inches) wide.
3. Arrange the melon slices on a serving platter, interleaved with slices of ham.
4. For the dressing, finely chop the stem ginger and place in a mixing bowl. Add the ginger syrup, oil, lemon juice and pepper and whisk together.
6. Pour the dressing evenly over the melon and ham. Cover and chill for ½ hour before serving.

PEACHES AND CREAM SALAD

Serves 4 as a starter
225 g (8 oz) full fat soft cheese
1-2 tablespoons single cream or milk (optional)
salt
freshly ground black pepper
100 g (4 oz) mixed nuts, chopped and toasted
lettuce leaves
4 ripe peaches or nectarines, halved and stoned, weighing together 500-600 g (1¼-1½ lb)
1 × 50 g (2 oz) jar caviar or lumpfish roe, to garnish (optional)

Preparation time: 10 minutes

PEARS IN STILTON

Serves 4 as a side salad or starter
150 ml (5 fl oz) plain unsweetened yogurt
100 g (4 oz) blue Stilton cheese
salt
freshly ground black pepper
1 small lettuce
4 ripe pears
1 bunch watercress, to garnish

Preparation time: 10 minutes

1. Blend the yogurt with half the blue Stilton cheese until smooth. Add salt and pepper to taste.
2. Arrange a bed of lettuce leaves on 4 individual plates. Core and slice the pears, arranging one pear on each plate.
3. Spoon the Stilton dressing over the pear slices and top with the remaining cheese, either crumbled or grated.
4. Garnish each plate with a few sprigs of watercress. Serve at once.

Variation:
For a more substantial salad, add a crisply grilled rasher of bacon, chopped or left whole, to each serving.

1. Beat the cheese until smooth and if necessary thin it down with a little cream or milk. Add salt and pepper to taste. Stir in half the nuts.
2. Divide the lettuce leaves between 4 individual plates, and place 2 peach halves on each plate.
3. Spoon some cream cheese filling into the centre of each peach half and sprinkle the reserved nuts over the top.
4. Garnish each serving with a spoonful of caviar or lumpfish roe, if liked.

Variation:
Use the same filling to stuff 8 thin or 4 thick slices of pineapple.

CLOCKWISE FROM THE BOTTOM Melon and Parma ham salad; Pears in Stilton; Peaches and cream salad

FENNEL AND APPLE SALAD

Serves 4-6 as a side salad
2 small bulbs fennel, about 450 g (1 lb)
4 small or 3 large dessert apples
50 g (2 oz) shelled hazelnuts, roughly chopped
150 ml (¼ pint) thick Mayonnaise (page 78)
5 tablespoons orange juice
salt
freshly ground black pepper

Preparation time: 15 minutes

1. Cut the fennel bulbs in half lengthways. Trim off the feathery green leaves from the tops and reserve for the garnish. Slice the fennel very finely and put in a large mixing bowl.
3. Quarter the apples, remove the cores, and cut into thin slices. Add the apples and chopped hazelnuts to the fennel.
3. Spoon the mayonnaise into a large bowl or jug, add the orange juice and blend until smooth. Add salt and pepper to taste.
4. Pour the dressing over the salad and toss until all the ingredients are thoroughly coated in dressing.
5. Garnish with the reserved fennel leaves. Serve as a side salad with cold roast meat or with whole, cold poached fish.

CRUNCHY GREEN SALAD WITH BLUE CHEESE DRESSING

Serves 4-6 as a side salad
100 g (4 oz) green cabbage
100 g (4 oz) broccoli
100 g (4 oz) courgettes
1 small green pepper
1 stick celery, thinly sliced
150 ml (¼ pint) Soured cream blue cheese dressing (page 79)

Preparation time: 25 minutes

1. Slice the green cabbage very thinly, discarding any core. Wash, drain and place in a mixing bowl.
2. Divide the broccoli into florets, cutting away the coarse central stalks and slicing down the thin stalks and heads. Wash, drain and add to the mixing bowl.
3. Top and tail the courgettes and slice as thinly as possible. Add to the bowl.
4. Cut the pepper into halves or quarters, remove the core and seeds, and slice very thinly. Add to the bowl with the prepared celery. Pour the blue cheese dressing over the vegetables and toss well.
5. Leave to marinate for 1 hour before serving. A
A Can be prepared several hours in advance, covered and kept chilled.

BREAD AND CHEESE SALAD

Serves 4 as a main salad
4 thick slices day-old bread (brown or white), weighing together about 100 g (4 oz)
150 ml (¼ pint) French dressing (page 78)
1 teaspoon fresh thyme leaves, or ½ teaspoon dried thyme
8 sticks celery, sliced crosswise
4 tomatoes, cut into wedges
225 g (8 oz) hard cheese, e.g. Lancashire, Double Gloucester, Cheddar, Edam
lettuce or endive (optional)
celery leaves, to garnish

Preparation time: 15 minutes

1. Cut the bread into cubes, about 2 cm (¾ inch) square, and place in a large bowl.
2. Mix the French dressing with the thyme and pour over the bread. Toss until all the bread is coated in dressing.
3. Add the celery and tomatoes and toss lightly.
4. Cut the cheese into small cubes or sticks and add to the salad. Ⓐ
5. Serve straight from the bowl, or on a bed of lettuce or endive, garnished with celery leaves.
Ⓐ Can be prepared several hours in advance, covered and kept chilled.

BEEF AND RADISH SALAD

Serves 4 as a main salad
450 g (1 lb) cold rare roast beef
1 bunch radishes, with leaves
50 g (2 oz) walnut halves, broken
1 small endive (optional)
Dressing:
4 tablespoons walnut or olive oil
2 tablespoons orange juice
1 tablespoon wine vinegar
salt
freshly ground black pepper

Preparation time: 15 minutes

1. Thinly slice the beef and cut into strips about 4 × 1 cm (1½ × ½ inch) and place in a bowl.
2. Select a few of the best radishes to make 'roses' for garnishing: with a small, sharp knife make long incisions running from the top of each radish to within 1 cm (½ inch) of the base. Leave in iced water for several hours, or overnight, to open out. Thinly slice the remaining radishes and add to the beef.
3. Add the walnuts to the bowl.
4. Mix all the ingredients for the dressing together and pour over the ingredients in the bowl. Toss until everything is well coated in dressing. Ⓐ
5. Arrange a bed of endive (if using) in a serving dish. Pile the beef and radish salad in the centre and garnish with the radish roses and radish leaves.
Ⓐ Can be prepared several hours in advance, covered and kept chilled.

Slice down each radish to within 1 cm (½ inch) of the base

Store in iced water until ready for use

FROM THE LEFT Fennel and apple salad; Crunchy green salad; Beef and Radish Salad

INCA SALAD

Serves 4 as a main salad or 6 as a starter
4 tablespoons French dressing (page 78)
few drops of Tabasco sauce
2 medium avocado pears
350 g (12 oz) potato, peeled and cooked
1 × 200 g (7 oz) can tuna fish, drained and flaked
1 lettuce (optional)
4 small fresh chilli peppers, or cucumber slices, to garnish

Preparation time: 10 minutes, plus chilling

1. To make a hot chilli dressing, pour the French dressing into a mixing bowl and blend in Tabasco sauce to taste.
2. Cut the avocado pears in half, remove the stones and peel. Cut the flesh into small cubes. Lightly toss the flesh in the dressing.
3. Cut the cooked potato into small cubes and add to the avocado with the flaked tuna fish. Toss gently, making sure that the avocado does not get mashed.
4. Line a serving dish or individual plates with lettuce leaves (if using) and pile the avocado salad on top.
5. Garnish with chilli flowers: with a small, sharp knife or scissors, make several long incisions starting at the top of each chilli and running to within 1 cm (½ inch) of the base. Leave in iced water for several hours, or overnight, to open up. Alternatively garnish with twists of cucumber.

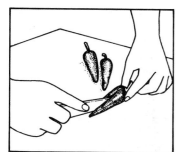
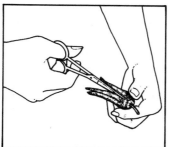

1. Cut along the length of each chilli to within 1 cm (½ inch) of the base

2. With scissors, cut down between existing cuts to make finer 'petals'

3. Store the 'flowers' in iced water until ready to use.

CEVICHE

Serves 4 as a main salad or 6 as a starter
750 g (1½ lb) firm white fish fillets e.g. cod, sole, whiting, halibut, plaice
4 tablespoons fresh lemon or lime juice
4 medium tomatoes
1 small green pepper
1 × 10 cm (4 inch) piece cucumber
2 tablespoons oil
1 tablespoon finely chopped or grated onion
1 tablespoon tomato ketchup
few drops of Tabasco sauce (optional)
salt
freshly ground black pepper
To serve:
1 small lettuce (optional)
slices of lime or lemon

Preparation time: 15 minutes, plus marinating

1. Skin the fish, cut into thin strips and place in a mixing bowl.
2. Pour over the lemon or lime juice and stir until all the fish is coated. Cover and chill for at least 2 hours until the fish has turned white and opaque and has the appearance of cooked fish.
3. Meanwhile prepare the vegetables. Skin the tomatoes, remove the seeds and chop the flesh into small dice.
4. Cut the pepper into quarters, discard the seeds and cut into 5 mm (¼ inch) dice. Cut the cucumber into slices and then into small dice.
5. When the fish has been marinated sufficiently, combine with the diced tomatoes, pepper and cucumber.
6. Mix the oil with the onion, tomato ketchup, Tabasco, salt and pepper, and stir into the salad. [A]
7. To serve, shred the lettuce finely (if using) and divide between individual plates or dishes. Spoon the ceviche on top, and garnish each serving with a twist of lime or lemon.
[A] Can be prepared up to 1 day ahead, covered and kept chilled.

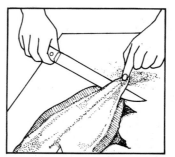

Sprinkle some salt under the tail, then insert a knife between the flesh and the tail

Slide the knife down the fillet, keeping the blade close to the skin

FROM THE LEFT Ceviche; Inca salad

RUSSIAN SALAD WITH TONGUE

Serves 4 as a main salad
350 g (12 oz) even-sized potatoes, scrubbed or peeled
225 g (8 oz) carrots, scraped or peeled
salt
100 g (4 oz) celery, sliced, or turnip, peeled and diced
225 g (8 oz) sliced beans or frozen peas
225 g (8 oz) thinly sliced cooked tongue
Dressing:
150 ml (¼ pint) Mayonnaise (page 78)
150 ml (5 fl oz) soured cream or plain unsweetened yogurt
1 tablespoon chopped gherkins
1 tablespoon capers
To garnish:
1 tablespoon capers
gherkin fans

Preparation time: 20 minutes, plus cooling
Cooking time: 20 minutes

1. Put the whole potatoes and carrots in a large saucepan and cover with cold salted water. Bring to the boil and simmer for 15-20 minutes until tender but not soft. Drain and leave to cool.
2. Blanch the celery or turnip with the beans in boiling salted water until just tender. If using frozen peas, boil them for 3-4 minutes in salted water. Drain the vegetables and leave to cool.
3. Cut the potatoes and carrots into dice and place in a mixing bowl with the prepared celery or turnip and beans or peas.
4. For the dressing, mix together the mayonnaise and soured cream or yogurt and stir in the gherkins and capers.
5. Pour the dressing over the prepared vegetables and toss to coat everything evenly. Ⓐ
6. To serve, arrange the slices of tongue around the edge of a platter. Pile the Russian salad in the centre and garnish with capers and gherkin fans.
Ⓐ Can be prepared up to 1 day ahead, covered and kept chilled.

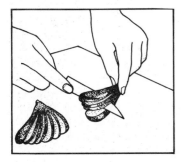

Slice the gherkin horizontally, cutting to within 1 cm (½ inch) of the thinnest end, then spread the fan 'leaves' apart

MARYLAND CHICKEN SALAD

Serves 4-6 as a main salad
1 chicken, about 1.5 kg (3 lb), cut into 6-8 joints
1 tablespoon seasoned flour
1 egg, beaten
50 g (2 oz) breadcrumbs
50 g (2 oz) butter
1 tablespoon oil
4 small bananas
450 g (1 lb) sweetcorn kernels, fresh, frozen or canned
1 bunch watercress, to garnish
300 ml (½ pint) Yogurt/soured cream dressing (page 79)

Preparation time: 30 minutes
Cooking time: 25-30 minutes

1. Coat the chicken joints in the seasoned flour, then in the beaten egg, and cover with breadcrumbs.
2. Heat the butter and oil in a large frying pan. Fry the chicken pieces slowly for 15-20 minutes, turning until browned all over and cooked through. Drain on paper towels and leave to cool. Ⓐ Reserve the oil for frying the bananas.
3. Cook the fresh or frozen sweetcorn in salted boiling water until tender, about 10 minutes, or according to pack instructions. Drain and leave to cool. Ⓐ Drain canned sweetcorn.
4. Peel the bananas and cut in half lengthways. Heat the oil and fry them quickly, turning once, until lightly browned. Drain and leave to cool.
5. Arrange the chicken pieces on a large platter and surround with the sweetcorn. Garnish with the fried bananas and watercress. Hand dressing separately.
Ⓐ The chicken and sweetcorn can be prepared up to 1 day in advance. Keep separate, cover and chill.

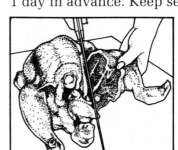

Cut off the legs

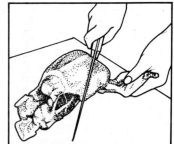

Cut off the wings

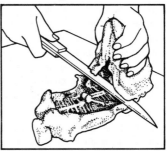

Cut off the breast

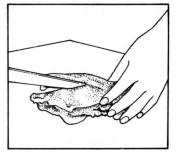

Divide the breast in two

SWEETCORN SALAD

Serves 4 as a side salad
450 g (1 lb) sweetcorn kernels, fresh, frozen or canned
salt
4 tablespoons corn oil
1 tablespoon wine vinegar
1 tablespoon Worcestershire sauce
1 tablespoon tomato ketchup
1 tablespoon soft brown sugar
1 tablespoon grated onion
50 g (2 oz) raisins
1 red or green pepper, finely chopped

Preparation time: 15 minutes
Cooking time: 10-15 minutes if using fresh or frozen sweetcorn kernels

1. Cook the fresh or frozen sweetcorn kernels in salted boiling water until tender, or according to pack intructions. Drain and leave to cool. If using canned kernels, simply drain.
2. Pour the corn oil into a mixing bowl. Add the vinegar, Worcestershire sauce, tomato ketchup, sugar and grated onion, and mix well.
3. Stir in the raisins and chopped pepper. Add the sweetcorn and stir until well mixed. A
4. This salad goes particularly well with hamburgers and barbecued foods.
A Can be prepared up to 2 days in advance, covered and kept chilled.

FROM THE TOP Sweetcorn salad; Maryland chicken salad

MULLED MUSHROOMS

Serves 4 as a side salad or starter
2 tablespoons olive or corn oil
2 onions, peeled, halved and thinly sliced
1 celery stick, thinly sliced
1 large garlic clove, peeled and crushed
2 rashers streaky bacon, rinded and chopped
150 ml (¼ pint) red wine
225 g (8 oz) tomatoes, skinned, quartered and seeded
1 tablespoon fresh thyme leaves, or 1½ teaspoons dried thyme
1 bay leaf
1 cinnamon stick (optional)
salt
freshly ground black pepper
450 g (1 lb) button mushrooms, washed
1 tablespoon fresh thyme leaves, to garnish (optional)

Preparation time: 10 minutes, plus chilling
Cooking time: 15 minutes

1. Heat the oil in a large saucepan. Add the onions, celery, garlic and bacon, and fry gently for 5 minutes, stirring occasionally.
2. Stir in the wine, tomatoes, thyme, bay leaf, cinnamon stick, salt and pepper. Bring to the boil, then lower the heat.
3. Cut any large mushrooms into halves or quarters, but leave the rest whole. Add the mushrooms to the sauce in the pan.
4. Simmer gently for 10 minutes. Leave to cool and remove the bay leaf and cinnamon stick. Chill for at least one hour. [A]
5. Serve sprinkled with the fresh thyme leaves. This salad is delicious as part of a buffet which includes cold roast meats.
[A] Can be prepared up to 1 day in advance, covered and kept chilled.

> Unless the skins are very tough or dirty, mushrooms do not need to be peeled. The simplest way of cleaning them is to wipe the caps with a damp paper towel, but if they are very gritty or sandy they may need washing. Do this as quickly as possible to preserve their texture and prevent them from becoming soggy. To store mushrooms keep them in an open plastic bag in the refrigerator. They should keep for 4-5 days.

LEMON AND THYME MUSHROOMS

Serves 4 as a side salad or starter
225 g (8 oz) large, flat mushrooms
1 small lemon
6 tablespoons olive oil
1 tablespoon fresh thyme leaves or 1 teaspoon dried thyme
1 tablespoon chopped fresh parsley
1 small garlic clove, crushed (optional)
salt
freshly ground black pepper

Preparation time: 10 minutes, plus marinating

1. Slice the mushrooms crosswise into long thin strips and arrange in a shallow serving dish.
2. Grate the rind of the lemon into a mixing bowl and add the squeezed juice.
3. Whisk in the olive oil, thyme, parsley, garlic and salt and pepper.
4. Pour the dressing over the mushrooms and leave to marinate for at least 1 hour. [A]
[A] Can be prepared several hours in advance, covered and kept chilled.

Variation:
For a more substantial salad add 225 g (8 oz) peeled prawns or flaked tuna fish.

SWEET AND SOUR CHINESE SALAD

Serves 4 as a side salad
2 tablespoons corn oil
1 tablespoon clear honey
1 tablespoon soy sauce
2 tablespoons lemon juice
100 g (4 oz) mushrooms, sliced
6 spring onions, chopped
100 g (4 oz) bean-sprouts
225 g (8 oz) Chinese leaves, coarsely shredded

Preparation time: 10 minutes

1. Pour the oil, honey, soy sauce and lemon juice to taste into a large bowl and mix until well blended.
2. Add the sliced mushrooms to the soy dressing and mix until well coated and browned.
3. Stir in the spring onions and bean-sprouts. Add the Chinese leaves and toss well. Serve as a side salad with pork chops, spare ribs or cold roast pork.

FROM THE TOP Sweet and sour Chinese Salad; Mulled mushrooms

RISOTTO SALAD

Serves 4 as a light main salad

2 tablespoons oil
4 rashers streaky bacon, rinded and chopped
1 medium onion, peeled and chopped
225 g (8 oz) chicken livers, chopped
1 garlic clove, peeled and crushed (optional)
225 g (8 oz) long or medium-grain rice
600 ml (1 pint) chicken stock
½ teaspoon dried oregano or marjoram
salt
freshly ground black pepper
1 × 200 g (7 oz) can sweetcorn, drained
150 ml (¼ pint) French dressing (page 78)
1 tablespoon chopped fresh parsley, to garnish

Preparation time: 10 minutes
Cooking time: 20 minutes

This chicken liver risotto is cooked exactly as a hot risotto but French dressing is stirred into the rice mixture while it is still hot to add extra flavour, and it is then allowed to cool.

1. Heat the oil in a large saucepan and fry the bacon and onion for 3 minutes.
2. Add the chicken livers and garlic. Fry for 2 minutes longer, stirring occasionally.
3. Stir in the rice and fry for 1 minute. Add the chicken stock, herbs, salt, pepper and sweetcorn. Bring to the boil.
4. Cover the pan and simmer for about 15 minutes until all the stock is absorbed and the rice is cooked.
5. Transfer the risotto to a bowl, pour half of the French dressing over while still hot and stir in well. Leave to cool. [A]
6. Just before serving stir in the remaining dressing and sprinkle with the chopped parsley. Accompany with a green salad.
[A] Can be prepared up to 1 day ahead, covered and kept chilled.

Variation:
Use brown rice rather than white. This will require the same amount of water, but will take about twice as long to cook. For perfect cooked rice, when all the water has evaporated and the rice is just tender, remove the pan from the heat and leave it (covered) for a few minutes. The rice will fluff up in its own steam.

Risotto salad; Provençal stuffed eggs

PROVENÇAL POTATO SALAD

Serves 4-6 as a side salad
1 × 50 g (2 oz) can anchovy fillets
½ teaspoon dried mixed herbs
1 teaspoon chopped fresh parsley (optional)
1 tablespoon olive oil
500 g (1¼ lb) potatoes, peeled and thinly sliced
1 small onion, peeled and thinly sliced
225 g (8 oz) tomatoes, thinly sliced

Preparation time: 20 minutes
Cooking time: 1-1¼ hours
Oven: 190°C, 375°F, Gas Mark 5

1. Put the anchovies with their oil in a basin. Add the mixed herbs and parsley and mash into a paste.
2. Take a 1.25 litre (2 pint) ovenproof dish, about 5 cm (2 inches) deep, and brush with oil.
3. Arrange a third of the potatoes over the base of the dish. Cover with half of the onion and half of the tomatoes and spread lightly with half of the anchovy paste. Repeat, and top with a layer of potato.
4. Brush the top with the oil, and bake for 1-1¼ hours in a preheated oven until the top is golden and the potatoes are cooked through. Leave to cool. [A]
[A] Can be prepared up to 1 day ahead, covered and kept chilled.

PROVENÇAL STUFFED EGGS

Serves 4 as a starter
50 g (2 oz) black olives, stoned
1 × 50 g (2 oz) can anchovy fillets, soaked in milk then drained (reserving the oil)
1 tablespoon capers
4 eggs, hard-boiled
4 tomatoes, sliced
1 tablespoon chopped fresh parsley
2 tablespoons French dressing (page 78)
4 black olives, stoned and halved, to garnish
shredded lettuce, to serve

Preparation time: 15 minutes

1. Place the olives in a mixing bowl or mortar. Add the anchovies with their oil and the capers and pound to a paste.
2. Shell the eggs and cut them in half lengthways. Scoop out the yolks and mix them into the paste.
3. Spoon some paste into the centre of each half egg and arrange the eggs around the edge of a serving dish.
4. Arrange a bed of shredded lettuce on a serving platter. Pile the tomato slices into the centre and sprinkle them with parsley and French dressing.
5. Garnish each half egg with half a black olive.

SALAD STUFFED PEPPERS

Serves 8 as a starter or 4 as a main vegetarian salad
175 g (6 oz) rice
300 ml (½ pint) water
salt
4 red, yellow or green peppers
225 g (8 oz) tomatoes, skinned and chopped
50 g (2 oz) chopped walnuts
50 g (2 oz) raisins
2 tablespoons chopped fresh parsley
4 tablespoons French dressing (page 78)
freshly ground black pepper
150 ml (¼ pint) water or stock

Preparation time: 20 minutes
Cooking time: 1 hour
Oven: 190°C, 375°F, Gas Mark 5

1. Put the rice in a saucepan with the water and a
little salt. Cover, bring to the boil, and simmer for
about 15 minutes until all the water has been
absorbed and the rice is just cooked.
2. Meanwhile, prepare the peppers: cut them in half
lengthways and discard the core and seeds.
3. When the rice is cooked, stir in the chopped
tomatoes, walnuts, raisins, parsley, French dressing
and salt and pepper to taste.
4. Spoon the rice salad into the pepper halves and
place in a roasting tin or ovenproof dish. Pour the
water or stock round the peppers.
5. Cover and bake in a preheated oven for about 45
minutes until the peppers are tender. Leave to
cool. A
A Can be prepared up to 1 day ahead, covered and
kept chilled.

Variations:
Many other autumn vegetables can also be stuffed:
Aubergines: Halve lengthways and scoop out the
cores. Sprinkle with salt and leave upside down for
30 minutes to drain. Rinse, stuff then bake for 1 hour
until tender.
Courgettes: Halve lengthways and scoop out the
cores. Stuff and bake for 30-45 minutes, depending
on size.
Round Courgettes: These are a new variety and are
ideal for stuffing. Slice off the tops and reserve these
as lids. Stuff, replace lids and bake as for Courgettes.
Onions: Peel and slice off the root ends so that they
will sit level. Simmer for 10 minutes, then drain.
Slice off the tops and reserve as lids. Pull out the
centres, stuff the cavities, replace the lids and bake
for 45 minutes.
Tomatoes: Use the Mediterranean variety. Slice off
the tops and reserve these as lids. Scoop out the
seeds, stuff and bake for 15-20 minutes until tender.

ORCHARD SALAD

Serves 4-6 as a side salad
grated rind and juice of 2 small oranges
1 tablespoon chopped fresh mint or parsley
salt
freshly ground black pepper
350 g (12 oz) firm pears
350 g (12 oz) dessert apples (e.g. Cox's, Worcesters)
100 g (4 oz) blackberries
50 g (2 oz) shelled hazelnuts (in skins), roughly chopped

Preparation time: 15 minutes

1. Place the orange rind and juice in a mixing bowl. Stir in the herbs and salt and pepper to taste.
2. Quarter and core the pears and apples. Cut each quarter crosswise into wedge-shaped slices. Add to the orange juice and toss well.
3. Add the blackberries and hazelnuts to the other fruit and toss all together. This salad goes well with rich meats such as pork and duck.

LEEK, ORANGE AND HAZELNUT SALAD

Serves 4-6 as a side salad
450 g (1 lb) leeks
2 medium oranges
4 tablespoons olive oil
salt
freshly ground black pepper
50 g (2 oz) hazelnuts, toasted and chopped

Preparation time: 10 minutes, plus marinating

If a milder flavour is preferred, the sliced leeks may be blanched in boiling water for 1-2 minutes before using.

1. Slice the leeks into rounds as thinly as possible. Wash well, then separate into rings and drain.
2. To make the dressing, grate the orange rinds into long thin strips and place in a large mixing bowl. Add the juice from the oranges, the olive oil and salt and pepper to taste.
3. Whisk the dressing together and then add the leeks to the bowl. Toss until all the leeks are coated in dressing. Stir in the chopped hazelnuts.
4. Leave to marinate for at least 1 hour to soften the leeks. Ⓐ This salad goes particularly well with chicken and lamb.
Ⓐ Can be prepared several hours in advance, covered and kept chilled.

CHICKEN SALAD VÉRONIQUE

Serves 4 as a main salad
4 tablespoons cooking oil
1 garlic clove, peeled (optional)
4 boned chicken breasts
50 g (2 oz) split or flaked almonds
150 ml (5 fl oz) soured cream
1 tablespoon white Vermouth or dry white wine
salt
freshly ground black pepper
1 head endive, to serve
225 g (8 oz) green grapes, halved, pips removed or whole seedless grapes

Preparation time: 20 minutes
Cooking time: about 10 minutes

1. Heat the oil in a frying pan and add the whole clove of garlic. Fry the chicken breasts on both sides for 5-10 minutes until golden brown and cooked through.
2. Remove the chicken from the pan and drain on paper towels. Add the almonds to the pan and fry gently, stirring constantly, until lightly browned. Remove from the pan and drain. Allow the chicken and almonds to cool. Reserve the cooking oil and allow to cool, discarding the garlic. Ⓐ
3. Spoon the soured cream into a basin and beat in the cold cooking oil, vermouth or white wine, and salt and pepper to taste. Add a little more vermouth or white wine if a sharper dressing is preferred. Ⓐ
4. Arrange a bed of endive leaves on a serving dish and place the cold chicken breasts on top.
5. Pour the dressing over the chicken and scatter with the fried almonds and grapes.
Ⓐ Chicken and dressing can be prepared up to 1 day ahead. Keep separate, cover and chill.

Variation:
This is a cold version of the classic hot French dish Chicken Véronique. It makes an excellent choice for a lunch party or buffet: it not only looks extremely attractive, but can be prepared well in advance. For ease of serving, the chicken breasts can be cut into bite-size pieces and folded into the soured cream dressing with the grapes and almonds. Transfer the salad to a shallow serving bowl lined with lettuce leaves and serve.

CLOCKWISE FROM TOP LEFT Orchard salad; Chicken salad véronique; Chicken liver ring salad; Leek, orange and hazelnut salad

CHICKEN LIVER RING SALAD

Serves 4 as a light main salad or starter

1 × 25 g (1 oz) packet aspic jelly powder
600 ml (1 pint) water
2 tablespoons dry or medium sherry
25 g (1 oz) butter
225 g (8 oz) chicken livers, roughly chopped
2 spring onions, trimmed and thinly sliced
1 carton mustard and cress, to garnish

Preparation time: 15 minutes, plus chilling and setting

1. Make up the aspic jelly with the water according to the pack instructions. Leave to cool until beginning to thicken but not set. Stir in the sherry.

2. Melt the butter in a frying pan. Fry the chicken livers for about 3 minutes, turning frequently, over a brisk heat. Leave to cool.

3. Pour 150 ml (¼ pint) of the aspic jelly into the base of a 900 ml (1½ pint) ring mould. Place in the refrigerator or freezer to set.

4. Sprinkle the spring onions on top of the set aspic jelly. Distribute the chicken livers evenly in the ring mould, then pour in the remaining aspic jelly to fill up the mould. Place in the refrigerator until set. [A]

5. To serve, turn out and surround with a garnish of mustard and cress.

[A] Can be prepared up to 1 day in advance, covered and kept chilled.

WINTER

LEEKS À LA GRECQUE

Serves 4 as a side salad or starter
300 ml (½ pint) water (or water and dry white wine mixed)
2 tablespoons olive oil
grated rind of 1 lemon
2 tablespoons lemon juice
1 shallot or small onion, peeled and thinly sliced
1 small stick celery with leaves
sprig of parsley
sprig of thyme or ¼ teaspoon dried thyme
1 bay leaf
¼ teaspoon salt
6 peppercorns
6 coriander seeds or ¼ teaspoon ground coriander
450 g (1 lb) leeks

Preparation time: 15 minutes
Cooking time: 30 minutes

If preferred the leeks may be sliced into 2 cm (¾ inch) pieces, rather than left whole. These will take less time to cook and might be more suitable for a side salad.

1. Pour the water, or water and wine, into a large saucepan and add the olive oil, lemon rind and juice, shallot or onion, celery and leaves, parsley, thyme, bay leaf, salt, peppercorns and coriander. Cover the pan, bring to the boil and simmer for 10 minutes.
2. Cut off the roots of the leeks and the ragged green leaves at the top, so that each leek measures about 18 cm (7 inches) long.
3. Make a long, lengthways cut in each leek, starting at the green end. Pull the leaves open and plunge the leeks, green ends first, into cold water to flush out any grit from the insides.
4. Place the prepared leeks in the simmering water, cover, and simmer for 10-15 minutes until the leeks are tender.
5. Remove the leeks from the pan with a slotted spoon and place on a serving dish.
6. Boil the remaining liquid to reduce to about 150 ml (¼ pint). Pour the liquid over the leeks (removing the herbs and spices if preferred). Leave to cool. [A]
[A] The leeks can be prepared up to 1 day in advance, covered and kept chilled.

MOUSSAKA SALAD

Serves 4 as a main salad
750 g (1¾ lb) aubergines, stalks removed
1 tablespoon salt
about 150 ml (¼ pint) oil
1 large onion, peeled and chopped
750 g (1½ lb) minced lamb or beef
1 teaspoon tomato purée
1 garlic clove, peeled and crushed (optional)
freshly ground black pepper
1 large tomato, thinly sliced
3 eggs
1 tablespoon fresh marjoram or ½ teaspoon dried

Preparation time: 20 minutes, plus standing
Cooking time: 30-50 minutes
Oven: 180°C, 350°F, Gas Mark 4

1. Cut the aubergines into thin slices about 3 mm (⅛ inch) thick. Put them in a colander and sprinkle with the salt. Stand the colander on a plate and leave to drain for 30 minutes to draw out the bitter juices.
2. Rinse the aubergine slices and pat dry.
3. Heat 3 tablespoons of oil in a large frying pan. Fry the aubergine slices until golden brown on both sides, adding a further 6 tablespoons of oil as necessary. Remove the slices with a slotted spoon.
4. Gently fry the onion in the last tablespoon of oil for 5 minutes. Add the minced meat and fry for 5-10 minutes, stirring until lightly browned. Add the tomato purée, garlic, and a little salt and pepper.
5. Lightly grease a 1.25 litre (2 pint) ovenproof dish, or 4 individual 300 ml (½ pint) dishes. Arrange the aubergine slices, overlapping, over the base and sides of the dish, reserving some for the top. Arrange the tomato slices on top.
6. Spoon the mince mixture into the dish. Beat the eggs with the marjoram, pepper and a little salt. Pour the eggs over the mince and cover with the remaining aubergine slices.
7. Bake for 30 minutes in a large dish and for 15-20 minutes in smaller dishes, until the top is golden and the egg is set. Leave to cool. [A]
8. Run a palette knife around the edge of the dish(es) and invert on to a serving plate. Accompany with endive leaves.
[A] Can be prepared up to 1 day ahead, covered and kept chilled.

Moussaka salad; Leeks à la Grecque

BROCCOLI NIÇOISE

Serves 4 as a light main salad or 6 as a starter
450 g (1 lb) broccoli or calabrese
1 × 200 g (7 oz) can tuna fish, drained and flaked
2 eggs, hard-boiled and shelled
1 × 50 g (2 oz) can anchovy fillets
8 small black olives, stoned
150 ml (¼ pint) French dressing (page 78)

Preparation time: 10 minutes
Cooking time: 10 minutes

1. Cut the broccoli into small spears and simmer in a little boiling salted water for 5-10 minutes until tender but still crisp. Drain and rinse under cold water to cool quickly.
2. When the broccoli is cold, arrange it over the base of a shallow serving dish or platter. Arrange the flaked tuna on top.
3. Cut the hard-boiled eggs into wedges and place on top with the anchovies and black olives. [A]
4. Pour the French dressing over the salad. For a main salad serve with French bread.
[A] Can be prepared several hours in advance, covered and kept chilled.

RED BEAN AND CALABRESE SALAD

Serves 4 as a side salad
225 g (8 oz) dried red kidney beans or 1 × 425 g (15 oz) can red kidney beans, drained
900 ml (1½ pints) water
150 ml (¼ pint) French dressing (page 78)
225 g (8 oz) calabrese or broccoli
2 sticks celery, thinly sliced
2 spring onions, thinly sliced

Preparation time: 10 minutes, plus soaking and marinating
Cooking time: 1-1½ hours

1. If using dried beans, soak them in the water overnight or pour on the same amount of boiling water and soak for at least 2 hours.
2. Bring the beans to the boil in their soaking water, boil rapidly for 10 minutes, then cover and simmer for 1-1½ hours until tender. Drain.
3. Divide the calabrese into florets.
4. Place the warm, cooked beans or canned beans in a mixing bowl and pour the French dressing over. Add the broccoli, celery and onions and toss well. [A]
5. Leave to marinate for a few hours before serving.
[A] Can be prepared up to 1 day ahead, covered and kept chilled.

Red bean and calabrese salad

Soused herring salad

SOUSED HERRING SALAD

Serves 4 as a starter
4 herrings, heads and fins removed, gutted and cleaned
salt
freshly ground black pepper
1 medium carrot, thinly sliced
1 medium onion, peeled and thinly sliced
1 eating apple, peeled, cored and sliced (optional)
6 peppercorns
2 bay leaves
150 ml (¼ pint) wine vinegar
150 ml (¼ pint) water

Preparation time: 10 minutes, plus cooling
Cooking time: 30-40 minutes
Oven: 180°C, 350°F, Gas Mark 4

1. Remove the backbones from the herrings without removing the tails. Flatten the fish out.
2. Sprinkle the flesh with salt and pepper and roll each herring up towards the tail. Put the herrings in a shallow ovenproof dish, tails pointing upwards.
3. Scatter the carrot, onion and apple slices over the fish. Add the peppercorns and bay leaves and pour the vinegar and water over.
4. Cover the dish and bake in a preheated oven for 30-40 minutes until tender. Leave to cool. **A**
A Can be prepared up to 1 day ahead, covered and kept chilled.

JERUSALEM SALAD

Serves 4 as a side salad
750 g (1½ lb) Jerusalem artichokes, washed but not peeled
salt
Dressing:
grated rind and juice of ½ lemon
4 tablespoons olive oil
1 tablespoon fresh thyme leaves
1 tablespoon chopped fresh parsley
freshly ground black pepper

Preparation time: 10 minutes
Cooking time: 15 minutes

1. Place the artichokes in a saucepan, cover with cold water and add some salt. Cover the pan, bring to the boil and simmer for about 15 minutes until the artichokes are just tender. Drain, peel off the skins, and leave to cool.
2. For the dressing, put the lemon rind and juice into a mixing bowl. Add the oil, thyme, parsley and salt and pepper to taste and whisk together.
3. Slice the cold artichokes and place in a serving bowl. Pour the dressing over the salad and toss well to make sure that all the slices are completely coated in dressing. **A**
A Can be prepared several hours in advance, covered and kept chilled.

WINTER ROOT SALAD

Serves 4 as a side salad
6 tablespoons orange juice
2 tablespoons wine vinegar
3 tablespoons oil
50 g (2 oz) raisins
225 g (8 oz) celeriac, peeled
225 g (8 oz) carrots, peeled
salt
freshly ground black pepper

Preparation time: 20 minutes, plus marinating

Remember that celeriac must be tossed in dressing as soon as it is peeled to prevent it turning brown.

1. Mix together the orange juice, vinegar and oil in a bowl. Add salt and pepper to taste, and the raisins.
2. Cut the celeriac and carrots into fine julienne strips and add to the orange dressing. Mix well until everything is thoroughly coated in dressing.
3. Cover and marinate for 1-2 hours before serving, tossing occasionally, to soften the celeriac. [A]
[A] Can be prepared up to 1 day ahead, covered and kept chilled.

TURNIP AND WATERCRESS SALAD

Serves 4 as a side salad or starter
750 g (1½ lb) turnips
2 tablespoons lemon juice
salt
freshly ground black pepper
1 large bunch watercress, stalks removed
1 tablespoon Dijon mustard
150 ml (¼ pint) Mayonnaise (page 78)

Preparation time: 15 minutes, plus marinating

1. Peel the turnips and grate coarsely into long thin strips. Alternatively, cut into julienne strips with a knife.
2. Place the strips of turnip in a mixing bowl. Pour the lemon juice over and add salt and pepper to taste. Toss and leave to marinate for about 30 minutes to soften the turnip. [A]
3. Roughly chop the watercress and add to the strips of turnip.
4. Mix the mustard with the mayonnaise and add to the salad. Toss well to coat the turnip strips and watercress thoroughly.
[A] Can be prepared several hours in advance, covered and kept chilled.

WINTER LEAF SALAD

Serves 4-6 as a side salad
½ head endive
1 large head chicory
1 head radiccio (red chicory)
1 bunch watercress
1 head celery leaves
4 tablespoons French dressing (page 78)

Preparation time: 10 minutes

1. Separate the endive into individual leaves, keeping the stems intact, and place in a salad bowl.
2. Slice the chicory crosswise into thin rings and add to the endive.
3. Separate the radiccio leaves and add to the salad bowl.
4. Cut off the coarse watercress stalks and separate the celery leaves. Add the watercress and celery leaves to the salad.
5. Just before serving, pour the dressing over and toss the salad until all the leaves are well coated.

CHRISTMAS COLESLAW

Serves 4 as a side salad
100 g (4 oz) red cabbage
100 g (4 oz) white cabbage
2 dessert apples, preferably red-skinned
50 g (2 oz) chopped nuts (e.g. walnuts, almonds, or brazils)
150 ml (¼ pint) Mayonnaise (page 78)
2 tablespoons French dressing (page 78)
1 tablespoon chopped fresh parsley, to garnish

Preparation time: 10 minutes

1. Shred both the cabbages very thinly and place in a large bowl.
2. Cut the apples into quarters, remove the cores and cut into very thin slices, keeping the skins on, and add to the cabbage.
3. Add the chopped nuts.
4. Mix the mayonnaise with the French dressing. Pour over the cabbage salad and toss until everything is thoroughly coated. [A]
5. Transfer to a serving dish and garnish with the chopped fresh parsley.
[A] Can be prepared several hours in advance, covered and kept chilled.

CRAB AND APPLE STUFFED AVOCADO

Serves 4 as a substantial starter or as a light main salad
4 tablespoons thick Mayonnaise (page 78)
2 tablespoons tomato ketchup
2 teaspoons lemon juice
salt
freshly ground black pepper
1 dessert apple
175 g (6 oz) crabmeat, fresh, frozen or canned, flaked
2 large avocado pears
1 small lettuce, to garnish

Preparation time: 10 minutes

1. Place the mayonnaise, tomato ketchup and lemon juice in a mixing bowl. Blend well and add salt and pepper to taste.
2. Quarter and core the apple and, keeping the skin on, coarsely grate it into the mixture. Stir well.
3. Mix in the crabmeat (if using canned crabmeat drain it first).
4. Cut the avocado pears in half and remove the stones. Spoon some filling on top of each avocado half. (If you are not serving the avocados immediately, make sure that all the flesh is covered by the filling so it will not come into contact with the air and go brown.)
5. Serve the avocados on individual dishes or arrange them on a platter, and garnish with lettuce leaves. Serve with a green salad as a light main meal.

BRUSSELS SALAD

Serves 4 as a side salad
225 g (8 oz) chestnuts
350 g (12 oz) Brussels sprouts
150 ml (¼ pint) French dressing (page 78)
salt (optional)
freshly ground black pepper (optional)

Preparation time: 20 minutes
Cooking time: about 15 minutes
Oven: 230°C, 450°F, Gas Mark 8

SPINACH NOODLE SALAD

Serves 6-8 as a starter or 4 as a light main salad
225 g (8 oz) green spinach noodles
salt
150 ml (¼ pint) French dressing (page 78)
small garlic clove, crushed (optional)
100 g (4 oz) mushrooms, thinly sliced
100 g (4 oz) cooked ham, thinly sliced
25 g (1 oz) grated Parmesan cheese

Preparation time: 5 minutes, plus cooling
Cooking time: 15 minutes

1. Add the noodles to a large pan of boiling salted water and cook for 10-15 minutes until tender but not soft (al dente). Drain.
2. Pour the French dressing into a large mixing bowl and add the garlic and mushrooms. Toss until the mushrooms are well coated.
3. Add the noodles while still warm and toss again.
4. Cut the ham into ribbons about the same width as the noodles, add to the salad and toss together. [A]
5. To serve, transfer to a large bowl and sprinkle with the Parmesan cheese.
[A] The salad can be made up to 1 day in advance, covered and kept chilled.

Variation:
The quantity of ham may be doubled to make a main course. Use 150 ml (¼ pint) Yogurt dressing (page 78) mixed with 2 tablespoons chopped fresh parsley instead of French dressing.

1. Slit the chestnut shells with a sharp knife and put the chestnuts on a baking sheet. Bake at the top of a preheated hot oven for about 15 minutes until the slits have opened.
2. While the chestnuts are still warm, remove the shells and inner skins. Roughly chop the chestnuts.
3. Trim off the stalk and outer ragged leaves from the sprouts and wash well.
4. Cut the sprouts in half lengthways. Place cut side down on a board and shred very thinly.
5. Place the shredded sprouts in a bowl and add the chopped chestnuts. Pour the French dressing over and mix thoroughly, adding salt and pepper if necessary. [A] Serve with cold roast turkey or chicken.
[A] Can be prepared several hours in advance, covered and kept chilled.

Crab and apple stuffed avocados; Spinach noodle salad

PINEAPPLE AND CHEESE SALAD BOATS

Serves 4 as a light main salad
1 medium pineapple, about 1 kg (2 lb)
225 g (8 oz) Cheddar cheese, cubed
½ cucumber, cut into cubes
50 g (2 oz) brazil nuts, sliced
4 tablespoons French dressing (page 78)
1 small lettuce, shredded
25 g (1 oz) shredded coconut, lightly toasted, to garnish

Preparation time: 15 minutes

TANGERINE AND HAZELNUT FLOWER SALAD

Serves 4 as a starter or side salad
4 large tangerines
50 g (2 oz) shelled hazelnuts with skins
225 g (8 oz) cottage cheese
50 g (2 oz) sultanas
salt
freshly ground black pepper
1 small lettuce, to serve

Preparation time: 10 minutes

1. With a sharp, pointed knife, cut a cross in the peel at the top of each tangerine and pull back the skin in four sections, leaving the fruit intact. Peel the skin back to make a case resembling the petals of a flower, keeping the skin joined at the stem end.
2. Remove the fruit and separate into segments, removing the excess pith. Chop the flesh into small pieces and place in a mixing bowl.
3. Roughly chop the hazelnuts and add to the tangerine pieces.
4. Stir in the cottage cheese, sultanas, and salt and pepper to taste.
5. Spoon the filling back into the tangerine skin cases. Place the tangerines on individual plates on top of a few lettuce leaves.

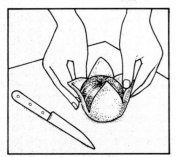 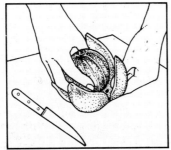

Pulling back the peel in four sections

Removing the fruit from the peel 'case'

1. Cut the pineapple into quarters, lengthways, keeping the stalk attached. Cut the flesh away from the skin and cut into cubes. Reserve the skins.
2. In a large bowl, mix the cubed cheese and cucumber with the pineapple and nuts. Pour the French dressing over and toss. [A]
3. Arrange the pineapple skin 'boats' on a serving dish or individual plates. Place some lettuce on top of each pineapple boat and pile the pineapple and cheese salad on top.
4. Sprinkle with the cooled toasted coconut.
[A] Filling may be prepared several hours in advance, covered and kept chilled.

WALDORF SALAD

Serves 4 as a side salad
3-4 red-skinned apples
1 tablespoon lemon juice
4 sticks celery, thinly sliced crosswise
50 g (2 oz) shelled walnuts, roughly chopped
100 g (4 oz) dates, chopped (optional)
150 ml (¼ pint) Mayonnaise (page 78) or Yogurt/soured
    cream dressing (page 79)
salt
freshly ground black pepper
To garnish:
1 red-skinned apple (optional)
1 tablespoon lemon juice
celery leaves

Preparation time: 15 minutes

1. Core and chop the apples and place in a mixing bowl. Pour the lemon juice over and toss to prevent the apples from going brown.
2. Add the celery, walnuts and dates.
3. Stir in the mayonnaise or soured cream dressing. Mix well and add salt and pepper to taste. [A]
4. Turn into a serving dish. Just before serving, core and thinly slice the apple for garnish (if using) and toss in the lemon juice to prevent browning. Garnish with the apple slices and celery leaves. This salad is good with cold meats.
[A] Can be prepared several hours in advance, covered and kept chilled.

Variation:
For a main course, serve the salad with 4 slices of cold roast pork. Alternatively, cube about 225 g (8 oz) cold pork and stir into the salad, adding a little more dressing if necessary.

CLOCKWISE FROM TOP LEFT Cauliflower polonaise salad; Waldorf salad; Pineapple and cheese salad boats; Tangerine and hazelnut flower salad

CAULIFLOWER POLONAISE SALAD

Serves 4-6 as a side salad

1 medium cauliflower
salt
6 tablespoons French dressing (page 78)
2 hard-boiled eggs, finely chopped
2 tablespoons chopped fresh parsley
freshly ground black pepper
50 g (2 oz) butter
small piece of garlic, crushed (optional)
50 g (2 oz) fresh breadcrumbs

Preparation time: 15 minutes
Cooking time: 1 minute

1. Separate the cauliflower head from the leaves, discarding the coarse stalk at the base. Shred the leaves thinly and place in a saucepan.
2. Divide the cauliflower head into florets and add to the pan with a little salt. Pour over enough boiling water to cover the cauliflower. Return to the boil and boil for 1 minute. Drain and leave to cool.
3. Pour the French dressing into a mixing bowl. Add the chopped egg to the dressing with the parsley and salt and pepper to taste. Mix well, then add the cauliflower and toss until well coated in dressing. [A]
4. For the topping, melt the butter in a pan, add the garlic and breadcrumbs and fry until golden brown, stirring frequently. [A]
5. To serve, place the cauliflower in a shallow serving dish and sprinkle with the fried crumbs.
[A] Cauliflower and crumbs can be prepared several hours ahead and kept chilled until required.

PILAFF AND SPICED CHICKEN SALAD

Serves 4 as a main salad with a green salad
1 tablespoon oil
1 medium onion, peeled and chopped
225 g (8 oz) long-grain rice
600 ml (1 pint) water or stock
50 g (2 oz) raisins
50 g (2 oz) dried apricots, chopped
50 g (2 oz) shelled walnuts, chopped
1 cinnamon stick or pinch of ground cinnamon
1 bay leaf
salt
freshly ground black pepper
150 ml (¼ pint) French dressing (page 78)
350 g (12 oz) cold chicken meat
150 ml (¼ pint) Curry dressing (page 79)
paprika, for sprinkling

Preparation time: 20 minutes, plus cooling
Cooking time: 20 minutes

1. For the pilaff, heat the oil in a large saucepan and fry the onion for 5 minutes.
2. Add the rice and cook for 1 minute, stirring. Pour in the water or stock and add the raisins, apricots, walnuts, cinnamon, bay leaf and salt and pepper. Bring to the boil, cover and simmer for about 15 minutes until the rice is cooked and all the water has been absorbed. Remove the cinnamon stick and bay leaf.
3. Stir in the French dressing and while the pilaff is still hot, press it into a 1.2 litre (2 pint) ring mould. Leave until cold. [A]
4. Cut the chicken into even-size pieces and combine with the curry dressing. [A]
5. To serve, turn the pilaff ring out on to a large serving plate and fill the centre with the curried chicken. Sprinkle a little paprika on to the chicken.
[A] Pilaff ring and spiced chicken can be made up to 1 day in advance. Keep separate, cover and chill.

MUSSEL SALAD

Serves 6 as a starter or 4 as a main salad
2 litres (3½ pints) fresh mussels
2 tablespoons oil
2 shallots or 1 small onion, peeled and thinly sliced or
   chopped
4 tablespoons dry white wine
salt
freshly ground black pepper
1 lettuce, shredded, to serve
2 tablespoons olive oil
1 tablespoon lemon juice
2 tablespoons chopped fresh parsley

Preparation time: 40 minutes
Cooking time: 10 minutes

If fresh mussels are not available, use 350 g (12 oz) shelled mussels, either canned or frozen, instead. Toss them in 150 ml (¼ pint) Lemon French dressing (page 78) and sprinkle with chopped parsley.
1. Discard any mussels that have broken shells or that do not close when tapped. Wash the remaining mussels well under cold running water.
2. Scrub each mussel, pull away the beards and scrape off any barnacles with a sharp knife. Continue washing in running water until all the mussels are thoroughly cleaned and the water runs clear. Drain.
3. Heat the oil in a large saucepan and gently fry the shallots or onion for 5 minutes until lightly browned.
4. Pour in the wine and add a little salt and pepper. Add the mussels. Cover the pan, bring to the boil and cook for 5 minutes, shaking the pan occasionally, until all the mussels have opened. Discard any that do not open.
5. Remove the mussels, reserving the liquid, and take them out of their shells. Boil the liquid to reduce to 150 ml (¼ pint) and leave to cool. [A]
6. Arrange the shredded lettuce over the base of a serving dish or individual plates. Place the mussels on top.
7. Mix the cooking liquid with the olive oil, lemon juice and parsley and pour over the mussels.
[A] The mussels can be prepared several hours in advance, covered and kept chilled.

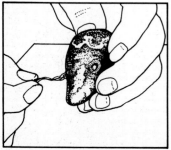
Pulling off the beards

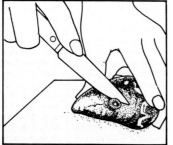
Scraping the shell clean

GADO GADO

Serves 4-6 as a side salad
100 g (4 oz) cabbage, shredded
100 g (4 oz) French beans, cut into 4 cm (1½ inch) lengths
100 g (4 oz) carrots, sliced
100 g (4 oz) cauliflower, divided into small florets
salt
50 g (2 oz) bean-sprouts
2 eggs, hard-boiled, shelled and sliced (optional)
50 g (1 oz) salted peanuts, to garnish
Peanut sauce:
4 tablespoons crunchy peanut butter
juice of 1 lemon
4 tablespoons water
few drops of Tabasco sauce
freshly ground black pepper

Preparation time: 15 minutes
Cooking time: 15-20 minutes

This is an Indonesian mixed salad with a peanut sauce.

1. Simmer the cabbage, beans, carrots and cauliflower separately in salted boiling water for a few minutes until tender but still crisp. Rinse under cold water to cool quickly. (There is no need to cook the bean-sprouts.) [A]
2. For the sauce, place the peanut butter in a mixing bowl. Gradually blend in the lemon juice and then the water until well mixed. Stir in enough Tabasco sauce to make quite a hot sauce, and add salt and pepper. [A]
3. Combine the cooked vegetables and the bean-sprouts and arrange in a shallow serving dish.
4. Lay the slices of hard-boiled egg over the top (if using) and pour the peanut sauce over the centre of the salad. Sprinkle with the salted peanuts.
[A] The vegetables can be prepared several hours in advance, covered and kept chilled until required. The peanut sauce can be prepared up to 1 day in advance, covered and kept chilled.

Variation:
This is an unusual salad idea. It is normally served alone as a cold dish, but it can be served with a spicy chicken or fish curry. The peanut sauce should be crunchy and of a thick pouring consistency. For an authentic Indonesian flavour, use coconut milk rather than water in the sauce. Make this by steeping 225 g (8 oz) desiccated coconut in 450 ml (¾ pint) warm water for 20 minutes. Strain off the water and squeeze the coconut grounds hard to extract all moisture.

CLOCKWISE FROM BOTTOM Mussel salad; Guacamole salad; Gado gado

GUACAMOLE SALAD

Serves 4 as a starter

4 tomatoes, skinned
2 tablespoons lemon juice
1 tablespoon grated onion
1 teaspoon chopped fresh coriander or ½ teaspoon
   ground coriander
¼ teaspoon Tabasco sauce
2 avocado pears

To garnish:

1 small lettuce
25 g (1 oz) packet potato or taco chips
sprigs of fresh coriander

Preparation time: 10 minutes

1. Cut the tomatoes into small dice about 5 mm (¼ inch) square and place in a mixing bowl.
2. Add the lemon juice, onion, coriander and Tabasco sauce and mix well.
3. Halve, stone and peel the avocados and cut the flesh into dice the same size as the tomatoes; add to the mixing bowl. Beat with a wooden spoon until the avocado has thickened the juices, but there are still cubes of avocado and tomato visible.
4. Arrange the lettuce leaves on 4 individual plates. Spoon the guacamole salad on top of the lettuce and garnish with coriander sprigs. Serve with crisps or taco chips, to dip into the salad.

TURKEY AND CRANBERRY SALAD

Serves 4 as a main salad
450 g (1 lb) cooked turkey meat
4 large sticks celery, thinly sliced crosswise
1 green pepper, cored, seeded and diced
50 g (2 oz) shelled walnuts, broken
150 ml (5 fl oz) soured cream
4 tablespoons cranberry sauce
1 tablespoon wine vinegar
salt
freshly ground black pepper
To garnish:
1 bunch watercress
few walnut halves

Preparation time: 15 minutes

1. Cut the turkey meat into cubes about 1 cm (½ inch) square and place in a mixing bowl.
2. Add the celery, pepper and walnuts.
3. Combine the soured cream with the cranberry sauce, vinegar, salt and pepper and mix well.
4. Pour the dressing over the turkey salad and toss until everything is well coated. [A]
5. Transfer to a serving dish and garnish with watercress and a few walnut halves.
[A] Can be made several hours in advance, covered and kept chilled.

HAM AND PINEAPPLE CORNETS

Serves 4 as a light main salad
4 large or 8 small slices cooked ham
225 g (8 oz) cottage cheese
1 × 225 g (8 oz) can pineapple slices in natural juice or fresh pineapple
1 small red pepper, cored, seeded and finely chopped
1 stick celery, chopped
salt
freshly ground black pepper
lettuce leaves, to garnish

Preparation time: 10 minutes

1. For the filling, put the cottage cheese in a bowl.
2. Drain the canned pineapple or peel and core the fresh pineapple, then chop and add to the cottage cheese. Add the prepared red pepper and celery. Season with salt and pepper to taste. [A]
3. Divide the filling between the slices of ham. Roll each slice into a cornet shape and arrange on a serving dish. Garnish with lettuce leaves.
[A] The filling can be prepared up to 1 day in advance, covered and kept chilled.

VITELLO TONNATO

Serves 4-6 as a main course
1 kg (2 lb) boned and rolled veal (e.g. leg, shoulder or breast)
1 onion, peeled and sliced
1 carrot, sliced
1 stick celery, sliced
1 bunch fresh herbs (parsley, thyme, bay leaf)
salt
freshly ground black pepper
2 tablespoons dry white wine, sherry or vermouth
Tuna mayonnaise:
200 ml (⅓ pint) Mayonnaise (page 78)
1 × 75 g (3 oz) can tuna fish in oil, undrained
1 tablespoon anchovy essence
1 teaspoon tomato purée
1 teaspoon lemon juice
salt
freshly ground black pepper
To garnish:
1 × 50 g (2 oz) can anchovy fillets
1 tablespoon capers
lemon slices

Preparation time: 20 minutes, plus cooling and chilling
Cooking time: about 1 hour

This is a popular Italian dish of cold sliced veal dressed with a tuna mayonnaise.

1. Place the joint of veal in a saucepan. Add the onion, carrot, celery, herbs and salt and pepper. Pour over enough cold water just to cover the veal and then add the wine.
2. Cover the pan, bring to the boil and simmer for about 1 hour until tender. Leave to cool in the stock.
3. For the tuna mayonnaise pound or liquidize all the ingredients together until smooth. (If the mayonnaise needs thinning add a little of the cooled veal stock.)
4. Thinly slice the veal. Spread each slice with a teaspoon of the tuna mayonnaise and arrange, overlapping, on a serving platter. Pour the rest of the mayonnaise over until all the slices of veal are covered completely.
5. Chill in the refrigerator for several hours or overnight to firm the mayonnaise.
6. To serve, garnish with the anchovy fillets, capers and lemon slices. This salad is ideal for a buffet lunch or dinner.

FROM THE TOP Vitello tonnato; Ham and pineapple cornets

DRESSINGS

FRENCH DRESSING

Makes 150 ml (¼ pint)
2 tablespoons wine vinegar or lemon juice
6 tablespoons oil (olive, sunflower, walnut or groundnut oil)
pinch of mustard powder (optional)
pinch of salt
freshly ground black pepper

Preparation time: 5 minutes

A mixture of oils may be tried, such as sunflower oil blended with a more exotic one, e.g. walnut oil. Half the amount made in this recipe should be enough to dress a large salad.

1. Place all the ingredients in a screw-top jar and shake vigorously until well blended. Shake again just before using. Alternatively, whisk together well in a small bowl until well blended.
2. The dressing will keep for 1 week or longer in a screw-top jar in a cool place.

Variations:
Add one or several of the following ingredients:
1-2 tablespoons chopped fresh herbs. Grated rind of half a lemon or orange. 1 small garlic clove, peeled (add whole for a subtle flavour or crush for a stronger flavour). ¼-½ teaspoon made French mustard.

THOUSAND ISLAND DRESSING

Makes 200 ml (⅓ pint)
150 ml (¼ pint) Mayonnaise (page 78) or soured cream
2 tablespoons milk
1 tablespoon tomato purée
1 tablespoon finely chopped red pepper
1 tablespoon finely chopped green pepper
1 tablespoon finely chopped gherkin
1 egg, hard-boiled, shelled and finely chopped (optional)

Preparation time: 10 minutes

1. Spoon the mayonnaise or soured cream into a mixing bowl. Slowly beat in the milk.
2. Stir in the tomato purée, then mix in the remaining ingredients. Cover and chill until required. Serve with fish or vegetable salads.

MAYONNAISE

Makes about 450 ml (¾ pint)
1 whole egg or 2 egg yolks
¼ teaspoon dry mustard
¼ teaspoon salt
1 tablespoon wine vinegar or lemon juice
300 ml (½ pint) oil (olive or salad oil or a mixture of the two)
1 tablespoon hot water

Preparation time: 10-20 minutes

Mayonnaise will keep, covered, in the refrigerator for a couple of days.

Using a blender:
1. Put the whole egg or egg yolks in the blender goblet and add the mustard, salt, and vinegar or lemon juice. Blend together at the lowest speed.
2. Remove the central cap in the goblet top, and with the blender running at its lowest speed, gradually pour in the oil. Add half the oil very slowly, when the mayonnaise will begin to thicken. Add the remaining oil in a steady stream.
3. Blend in the water. Taste the mayonnaise; if necessary add a little more vinegar or lemon juice.

By hand:
1. Stand a mixing bowl on a folded cloth to keep it steady while mixing.
2. Put the whole egg or egg yolks in the bowl and add the mustard, salt and a little of the vinegar or lemon juice. Using a wooden spoon, small wire whisk or hand-held electric beater, beat well.
3. Still beating, start adding the oil very slowly, drop by drop, until half the oil has been added and the mayonnaise begins to thicken.
4. Add the remaining vinegar. Pour in the remaining oil in a thin, steady stream, whisking constantly, until the mayonnaise is very thick. Add the water. If the mayonnaise becomes too thick to add all the oil, whisk in the hot water and then whisk in the remaining oil.

Variations:
Green Mayonnaise: To 300-450 ml (½-¾ pint) mayonnaise add one of the following: 1 bunch (about 50 g (2 oz)) watercress, coarse stalks removed, or about 50 g (2 oz) sorrel or cooked spinach, well-drained. Roughly chop and blend until smooth.
Anchovy Mayonnaise: To 300-450 ml (½-¾ pint) mayonnaise add 1 × 50 g (2 oz) can anchovy fillets with their oil and 1 tablespoon tomato purée. Blend until smooth.
Garlic Mayonnaise: To 300-450 ml (½-¾ pint) mayonnaise add 1-2 crushed garlic cloves.

CURRY DRESSING

Makes 450 ml (¾ pint)
1 tablespoon oil
1 small onion, peeled and chopped
1 tablespoon curry powder
150 ml (¼ pint) stock
1 tablespoon apricot jam
1 teaspoon lemon juice
150 ml (¼ pint) Mayonnaise (page 78)
150 ml (5 fl oz) plain unsweetened yogurt or soured cream

Preparation time: 15 minutes
Cooking time: 12 minutes

1. Heat the oil in a saucepan and fry the onion gently for 5 minutes until softened but not browned.
2. Add the curry powder and cook for 2 minutes, stirring continuously.
3. Stir in the stock and bring to the boil. Add the apricot jam and lemon juice and simmer for 5 minutes. Leave to cool.
4. Stir the mayonnaise and yogurt into the cold curry sauce. Mix well and add salt and pepper to taste. Serve with root vegetables or cold chicken salads.

YOGURT/SOURED CREAM DRESSING

Makes about 150 ml (¼ pint)
150 ml (5 fl oz) plain unsweetened yogurt or soured cream
1 tablespoon white wine vinegar or lemon juice
salt
freshly ground black pepper

Preparation time: 5 minutes

1. Put the yogurt or soured cream in a small mixing bowl and beat well.
2. Stir in the vinegar or lemon juice, salt and pepper. Alternatively liquidize all the ingredients together. To keep the dressing for a few days, cover and store in the refrigerator.

Variations:
Herb: Stir in 2 tablespoons chopped fresh herbs (watercress, parsley, chives, thyme, basil, tarragon).
Blue Cheese: Stir in 2 tablespoons crumbled blue cheese (e.g. blue Stilton, Danish blue, Roquefort).
Cucumber and Mint: Coarsely grate a 4 cm (1½ inch) piece of unpeeled cucumber and stir it into the dressing with ½ teaspoon dried mint or 1 tablespoon chopped fresh mint.

FROM THE TOP Mayonnaise; French dressing; Thousand Island dressing; Curry dressing; Yogurt/Soured cream dressing

INDEX